Natalia Tolbatova
Co-author Avgusta Udartseva

Easy Flute Lessons
for Beginners

Theory, Practice and 42 Songs.
For Kids 12+ and Adults.
With Online Video and Audio

ISBN: 978-1-962612-18-0

The flute photo on the cover and p. 9; p. 15 — © LovePik, 30000006434
Picture design p. 1 — © Daniel Oravec / depositphotos
Photo p. 14 — © Yamaha Corporation / Wikimedia Commons
Picture design p. 37; p. 87 — © brgfx / Freepik

For any questions, comments or suggestions, email us at:
avgustaudartseva@gmail.com

CONTENTS

Part 3

Introduction

The flute is a monophonic instrument which means that it uses a single line of melody. It is a very expressive and mesmerizing instrument associated with birdsongs, the murmuring of a clear stream, the crystal glitter of snowflakes, magic and love. The sound of the flute is suitable for the embodiment of a wide variety of human feelings and experience: joy and sadness, excitement and tragedy, inspiration and all-consuming sorrow, transcendence and passion. It is true that the flute is a complex instrument in how it is made, but it has a very attractive, melodious tone. Learning to play the flute is not as difficult as it seems. Trust me, it is a truly fascinating process! There are many melodies that are written for the flute and are its signature features. Still, it can likewise be said that almost any instrumental or vocal melody can be played on the flute, which will make it radiate with new colors! Additionally, it has been scientifically proven that regular flute lessons have a positive effect on a person's concentration and health. The process of playing helps create resistance to the exhaled air flow, which in turn helps develop the alveoli of the lungs, lung tissue, as well as increase the volume of the lungs themselves.

In this book, you will learn everything you need to know to start playing the flute. You will learn about the varieties of flute, its components, how to hold it and the nuances of sound production. In fact, the information presented in this book will be useful not only for the purpose of learning to play the flute but will also introduce you to music theory in general.

We've also prepared 42 popular pieces of music that will help you happily master the instrument and learn to read sheet music. We have also included basic music theory and exercises for mastering flute technique. This should help you get a feel for and master the basics of playing the instrument. Classical and jazz tunes are selected on a task-specific basis for step-by-step mastery of the instrument. The book includes songs with lyrics to help you work on proper sound production and phrasing. We have also prepared accompaniments to 10 songs, which will give you the opportunity to learn to play the flute with accompaniment. Who knows, maybe it will inspire you to start your own band one day! The lessons in the self-study book are extensive. How long it will take you to master the material depends on your preparation. Invest more time into practicing. Do not hurry to move on to the next lesson until you have mastered the previous one. Go back repeatedly. Watch the training videos in their entirety (they are short).

The flute is also unique in that its music blends beautifully with other instruments in an orchestra while keeping its own personality. I hope that this book will help you figure out all the features of flute playing, so that you can play this amazing instrument to the fullest!

Natalia Tolbatova

PART 1

About the Flute

For any questions, comments or suggestions, email us at:
avgustaudartseva@gmail.com

1. The History of the Flute Use

History of Emergence and Ancient Flutes

Many millennia ago, people discovered that various objects could produce sounds. Hollow bones, shells with holes drilled in them, pods coiled into tubes, tree leaves, reeds — all these objects produce sounds when you put them close to your mouth and blow into them. All kinds of wind instruments, including flutes, are descended from pipes, whistles and horns. Legend has it that a man invented the flute when he heard the sound of a broken reed stalk in the wind, cut a tube out of the stem, made holes in it and began to play it. This instrument got its name from the Latin word *flatus,* which means "blowing". According to the ancient Greek myth, Pan, the god of forests and fields and patron of shepherds, fell in love with the nymph Syrinx. The nymph appealed to the river god for help, and the god turned her into a reed, from which Pan made a 'sweet-sounding' flute. In Greece, the flute was called the Syrinx and it was the most popular instrument.

Longitudinal, transverse and multi-barrel flutes originated in ancient times in different countries at the same time. The sound was produced by the friction of an air jet against the sharp edge of the labial opening. According to the latest hypotheses, Asia is thought to be the birthplace of the transverse flute. In ancient China musicians played longitudinal clay flutes *(xiao),* variants of Pan's flute with 12 bamboo shafts *(paixiao),* transverse flutes with 3–6 playing holes *(chi)* and short transverse flutes *(yue).* In the Middle Ages, the longitudinal and transverse flutes were in vogue in instrumental ensembles at royal courts. Their sound was pleasant, soft, but very weak, inexpressive, uneven in strength and not always accurate in pitch, so performers were constantly trying to improve the design of the instrument.

The Invention of the Modern Flute

By the end of the 17th century, French craftsmen had improved the transverse flute, which had come from the East, giving it a more expressive and emotional sound, and only then did conductors find it possible to introduce the flute into the orchestra and give it separate solo numbers. Between 1832 and

1847, the great master Theobald Böhm rethought the design of the instrument and improved the mechanism, which is still in use today.

Where the Flute is Currently Used

The flute is used in symphony, wind and other types of orchestras, in chamber music, and very often as a solo instrument. Some schools have brass bands where students learn to play the flute and often perform in the orchestra or as soloists at school events. In addition to modern orchestral instruments, folk flutes continue to exist in various countries.

2. Getting to Know Your Flute

What is a "Concert" Flute?

Concert flute (often referred to simply as 'the flute') is a labial woodwind instrument where the primary source of vibration is an air jet that, when blown into the instrument, splits against the inner edge of a part of the instrument called the labium (Latin *labium* — lip). Regardless of the material of the flute body, it is traditionally categorized as a woodwind instrument.

The Flute Family

The piccolo (small flute) is a smaller version of the flute that plays the sounds of the upper register. It is written an octave below the actual sound. Together with concert and alto flute it is used in symphony, wind and other types of orchestras, in chamber music, and sometimes as a solo instrument. The piccolo flute is usually used in orchestral music to provide a bright and piercing sound, especially in the high register. The proper piccolo flute was designed in the eighteenth century and at the turn of the eighteenth and nineteenth centuries entered the symphony orchestra, where it became one of the highest register instruments. Military and brass bands of the 19th century often used piccolo flutes in D-flat (commonly used in U.S. brass bands) or E-flat, but today such instruments are extremely rare.

Compared to the concert flute, the piccolo has a sharper, whistling sound. The design of the key mechanism is the same, but the cross-section of the barrel is inversely conical. The length is about 12 inches (half of the length of the concert flute). It consists of a head and a body. It is usually made of metal, wood and plastic.

Alto flute (Ital. *flauto contralto*; Fr. *flûte alto*; Germ. *Altflöte*) — a variation of the modern flute. It was designed by Theobald Böhm around 1854. Most often it will be in the key of G. Less often you might see it in F, it is played a fourth or fifth below what is written. It is theoretically possible to extract higher sounds, but they are hardly ever used in practice. The tone of the instrument is full and wide and is even more beautiful in the lower register. The sound of the instrument in the lower register is brighter and fuller than that of the concert flute, but it is only achievable when played no louder than *mezzo forte*. The middle register is flexible in nuance, full sounding; the upper register is sharp, less tone colored than the flute, the highest sounds would be difficult to play on the piano.

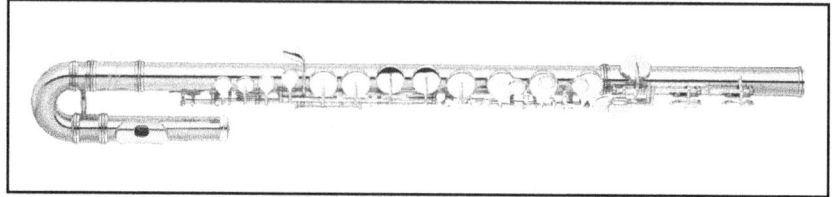

Together with the concert and piccolo flute, the alto is part of the symphony orchestra. It is comparable in terms of its parts and playing technique to the regular flute but has a longer and wider tube and a slightly different key system. The fingering is the same. Breath is used up more quickly on the alto flute.

Great Flutists of Different Countries

Johann Joachim Quantz (1697–1773, Germany); Michel Blavet (1700–1768, France); Giuseppe Gariboldi (1807–1882, Italy); Franz Doppler (1821–1883, Austro-Hungary); Karl Doppler (1825–1900, Hungary); Georges Barrere (1876–1944, USA); Geoffrey Gilbert (1914–1989, Great Britain); Julius Baker (1915–2003, USA); Aurèle Nicolet (1926–2016, Switzerland); Shigenori Kudo (1986, Japan).

Parts of the Flute

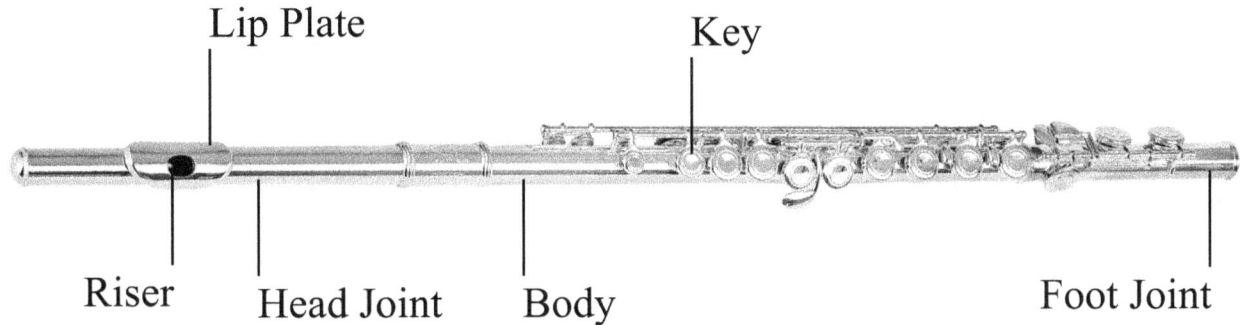

The transverse flute is generally a compound cylindrical tube consisting of three parts: the head joint, body, and foot joint. At one end of the instrument, which is closed, there is a side opening for blowing in and directing the flow of air.

The head joint is an indispensable part of the flute. It determines 70% of the sound strength and tone characteristics of the instrument. The body of the head is made in the form of a conical tube. Inside it, on the left end, there is a cork. Its position affects the tuning of the instrument. The position of the cork in the flute head is checked and tuned by a flute repair professional. Head joints can be both straight and curved (U-shaped and drop-shaped waveline, used for teaching small children, since it makes the instrument shorter). On the head joint of the flute there is the lip plate. It has an embouchure hole for blowing air into the instrument. The tube that connects the lip plate to the barrel of the flute head is called the riser. The walls of the riser form a specially engineered angle with the surface of the lips, which allows the air jet to swirl to produce the flute sound. Since the size and shape of the riser are key elements in creating the overall sound in the head joint (and therefore the flute itself), manufacturers make this crucial part of the instrument from a variety of materials and can coat it in silver, gold, or even platinum.

The flute's body and foot joint have a complex system of keys that close and open the holes on its body to adjust the pitch of the sounds. The body of the flute can be of two types: when the keys form a single line ("in-line") and when the G key is extended forward (not "in-line"). The keys are also of two types: open, with resonators, and closed, without resonators.

The foot joint of the concert flute can be of two types: the C joint, in which the lower sound is the C of the fourth octave; and the B joint, which sounds the B note of the third octave.

The range of the transverse flute is over three octaves, from the C of the fourth octave to the C of the seventh octave and even higher.

The notes are written in the treble clef and correspond to the pitch of the instrument.

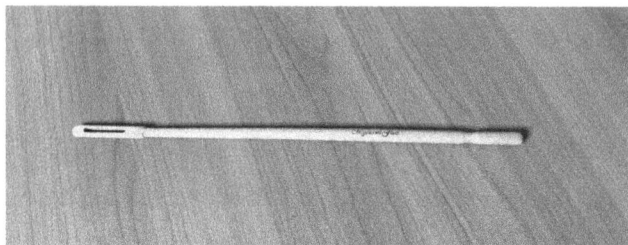

The flute outfit will most likely include a wooden, plastic or metal cleaning stick. It will help you take care of your flute.

A miniature sheet music stand can be attached to the flute head. If you might happen to be playing outdoors, this will come in handy to use as you won't have to memorize a huge number of notes.

German and French System Flutes and Their Differences

Visually, the differences between French and German flutes are almost invisible. The key ring holes are identical, but there are differences in the fingering of the notes. On a French system flute, the B key will come second from the head and the B-flat key will come first; on a German system flute, the B key will come first and the B-flat key will come second. Also, in the French system flute G-sharp is taken by pressing a special lever for the little finger of the left hand, while in the German system flute this lever is designed to take the G.

And one more thing. The French system flutes alone have the so-called E-mechanics — for easier and better-sounding E note in the sixth octave. Two neighboring keys (the G key and the one nearest to it on the lower joint) in flutes without E-mechanics are connected, while in the ones with E-mechanics they are separated, plus a small lever is added. German system flutes do not need E-mechanics because of how they are made.

16

Which Flute Should I Buy?

The flute is an instrument that has many different models and characteristics. One of the key aspects when choosing a flute is the material of the body. This parameter significantly affects the sound properties of the instrument and its durability. Modern flutes are most often made of nickel silver, that is nickel or brass alloys that are silver-plated on top. They combine durability and affordability, making these types of flutes an excellent choice for beginning musicians. Nickel plating and silver plating prevent corrosion of the instrument, which ensures the flute's longevity, but nickel can cause an allergic reaction in some people. Flutes are also made of silver. It provides a brighter and clearer sound, but such instruments are more expensive. A flute made of nickel silver (or *Neusilber*) with a silver head can be an affordable option, while also being pleasant and noble.

The choice of flute body material depends on the individual needs of each musician. Beginning musicians are recommended to choose a flute made of nickel silver to avoid overpaying for expensive and more difficult to maintain options. Experienced musicians can be advised to choose a silver flute, which will provide the best sound results.

Take note! For the initial period of learning to play the flute, it is better to choose an instrument with closed keys. The keys should not be arranged in one line, and should have a C joint as it is easier to play. For children and smaller folks there are flute models with a curved head which makes it easier for their hands to reach the needed position.

How Do I Check the Quality of a Flute Before I Buy It?

The first step in choosing a flute is to check the condition of the body and coating. They should be smooth over the entire surface, without dents, scratches or corrosion. Next, check the key system. Each key should move freely, without sticking, and there should be no other obstructions.

If you're ready to buy a new instrument, you might choose a student version from such reputable brands as Armstrong, Gemeinhardt, Burkart&Phelan, Selmer, Yamaha, Miyazawa, Muramatsu. A cheaper flute may seem to be of good quality at first glance, but over time you may have serious problems with the operation of the mechanism, or the keys on the inside of the pads may crack. Since instruments from reputable manufacturers are already established, often buying even a used Armstrong or Gemeinhardt instrument can be a good and reliable choice compared to a flute from an unknown manufacturer. In most cases, used instruments look and function quite well. They are typically sold by musicians. They may just be trading the older instrument to buy a new one.

If you decide to buy an instrument that has been used before, but you have doubts about its quality, you can check it for mechanical defects by contacting a flute repair professional. Perhaps music schools or music stores can tell you where to find a reliable repairman. Also, some flute repairmen may sell the instruments themselves. They perform maintenance and then put them up for sale.

When buying an instrument offhand, you should pay attention to the seller. Be sure to talk to them — the seller should know the history of the instrument, its characteristics and features. The more detailed and open your dialog is, the more confident you will be in making your decision. When choosing a flute, it is important to pay attention not only to its appearance, but also to its sound quality, because the pleasure you will get from playing the instrument will depend on it. Ideally, if you have the opportunity, ask the seller to make a video for you or perhaps to play the full scale on the instrument you are interested in. You want to make sure that you will also be able to play it as you start learning.

3. Before You Start

Preparing Your Flute

When sold, the flute comes in a special case that makes it easy to store and transport. The kit usually includes a cleaning stick and a cloth for cleaning the instrument inside and out. If necessary, you can choose and buy a music stand separately to suit your needs.

Putting the Parts Together

Take the instrument out of its case, inspect the joints and remove any dirt from them. The cleaner they are, the easier it will be to assemble the flute and, most importantly, the easier it will be to disassemble after playing. It is recommended that you periodically wipe the joints with a lightly moistened cloth. Insert the head joint of the flute into the main part (or body) from the wider side, and attach the foot joint from the other side; join the flute parts smoothly, with light rotating movements, avoiding misalignment. The fact is that the metal from which the flute is made is rather soft and thin, so try not to put extra effort when assembling and disassembling it. Pay special attention to the careful treatment of the key mechanisms.

Turn the flute head joint so that the hole in the lip plate is in line with the body keys. This can be easily checked by looking at the flute from the joint side. The manufacturer sometimes puts notches on the body and head joint of the flute to make it easier to find the correct position of the head. If you do not have such marks on your instrument, you can apply them yourself, for example, with small strokes of nail polish.

The position of the joint should be such that the key stem on the joint aligns with the middle of the nearest key on the body.

1)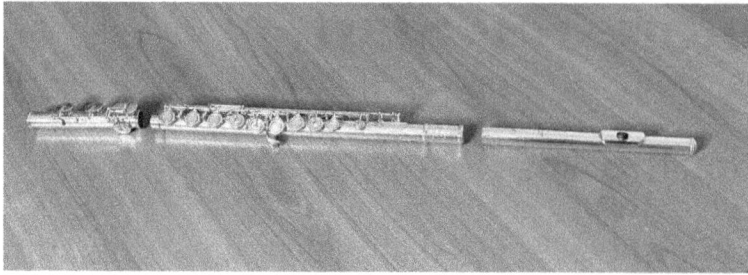

Watch the video

Putting the Flute Together

2)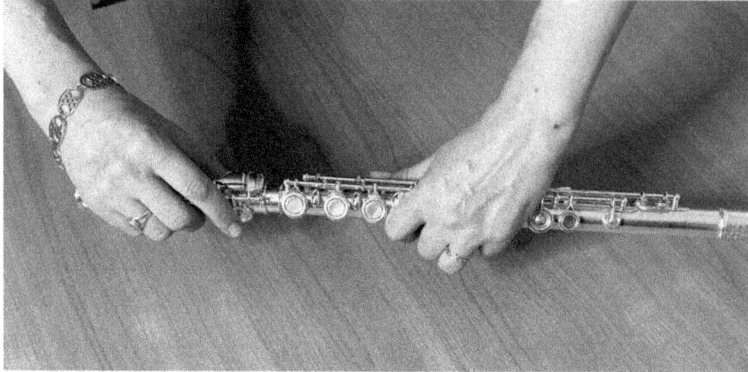

3)

4)

5)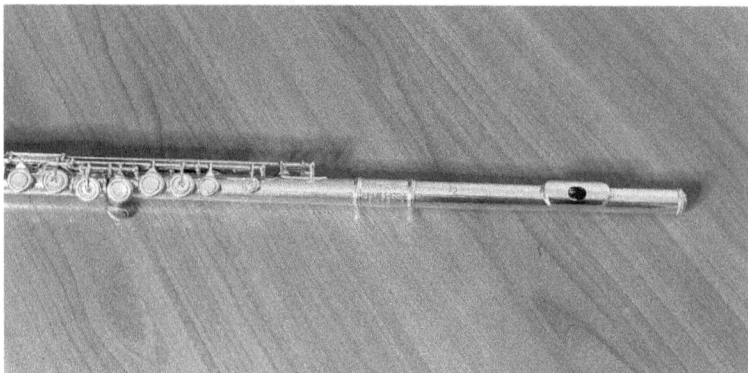

Taking Care of Your Instrument

Proper flute care is not only the way to keep your instrument in top condition, but also to ensure that you get the best sound out of your instrument. In this section, we'll go over some basic flute care tips.

Don't drop or swing your flute! Instead, handle it with care and protect it from getting hit. Take care not to deform the instrument. If you place the flute on an uneven surface, it may fall and become deformed, so place the instrument correctly: on a flat surface with the keys facing up. Do not place the transverse flute on its keys. Do not place the flute where it can be sat on or tipped over by pets.

Observe climate conditions such as temperature, humidity, etc. Keep the instrument away from heat sources such as heaters. Also, do not use or store your flute in places where it can be exposed to extreme temperatures or humidity. This can affect the balance of connections and the alignment of holes and keys, which can cause problems when playing the instrument.

Before using the flute or after using it, always store the instrument in its case. This helps prevent instrument damage and protects it from dust and dirt. The flute should be stored in a dry place to prevent the possibility of corrosion on the surface of the instrument.

Clean your flute after each use. This is one of the most important aspects of instrument care! You can use a special flute cloth, a cotton handkerchief, or a thin non-woven cloth for cleaning. Start by removing any saliva residue from the head and body, then gently wipe all parts of the instrument until all dirt and dust is removed. Metal polishing products remove a thin layer of metal plating, making the plating thinner over time. Please keep this in mind when using a metal coating polishing product.

1)

2)

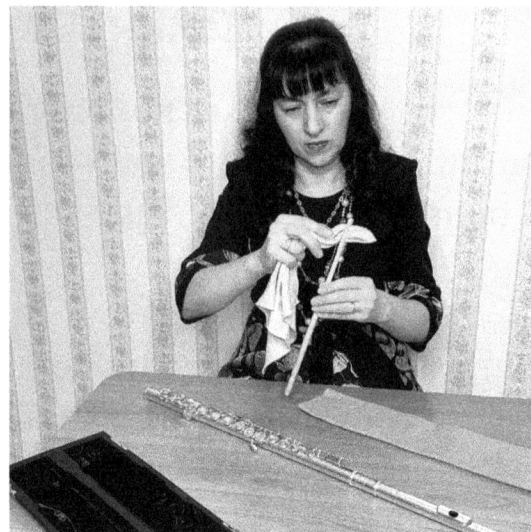

3)

4)

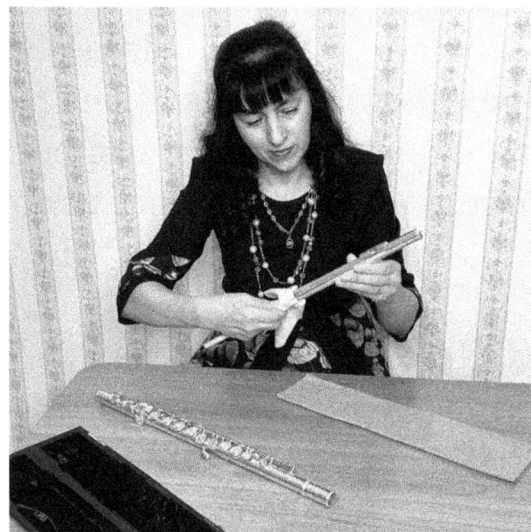

5)

6)

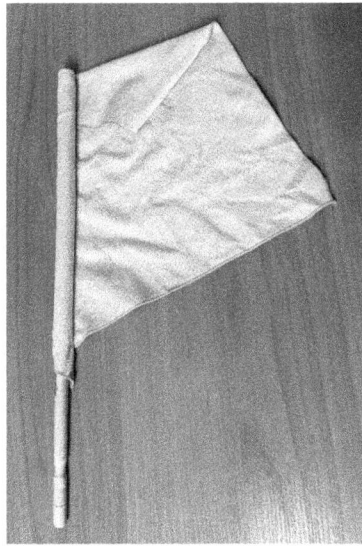

Check the condition of the keys. If you see any problems, do not try to fix them yourself, do not turn any screws in the mechanism, otherwise you may dislocate the keys. This can turn your flute into an artifact. It is best to contact a professional flute repair shop.

Never leave the flute in a car. The temperature in a car can vary significantly depending on the weather conditions. This can cause deformation of the body or other damage to the instrument.

Have your flute professionally cleaned and serviced regularly.
Even with proper care of your instrument, sooner or later it will need to be professionally serviced. It is recommended to have it serviced once every year or two years (depending on the frequency of use). Professional cleaning will help remove deeper clogs and dirt, as well as check the condition of the keys and keypads.

By following these basic flute care rules, you will not only keep your instrument in great condition, but you will also get the best sound out of your instrument. Don't forget professional maintenance and cleaning to ensure long life for your instrument.

4. Producing your First Sound on the Flute Head Joint

The word "embouchure" comes from "*bouche*", the French word for mouth. Basically, it defines how a person tenses the facial muscles and positions the lips when playing the flute. To form the correct sound, pull your lips slightly forward and feel how the tender inside part of your lips comes close together. Imagine as if you were going to say "pooh". This position of the embouchure will allow you to form an opening between your lips as needed, from wide to very narrow, like the eye of a needle.

The first thing you need to learn is to make the sound using the flute head joint without connecting it to the body. This is so that you can focus all your attention on making the sound and not be distracted by the need to hold the instrument. Stand in front of a mirror close enough to see your face and lips. Hold the flute head using both hands, position it horizontally with the open edge to the right and the lip plate with the embouchure hole on top. Place the rounded part of the lip plate against your lips, leaving the opening in a position parallel to the floor. Look in the mirror at your lips and the lip plate, making sure that the opening in the lip plate is pointing upwards, not towards the mirror and not pulled hard against your lips. You need enough room to blow air in (the photo shows how much the lower lip should cover the embouchure hole). I should remind you that you need to bring your lips together to the center, forming the "pooh" sound, not tense, but not completely relaxed either.

To accurately align the middle of the flute's embouchure hole with the center of your lips, you can use the following trick: turn the hole so that it faces you, feel its center with the center of your lower lip, then turn it away from yourself so that it is exactly in its place as in the photo — in the middle of the gap between your lips. Take the flute head joint away from your lips and then press it back again. Practice it enough for it to become automatic.

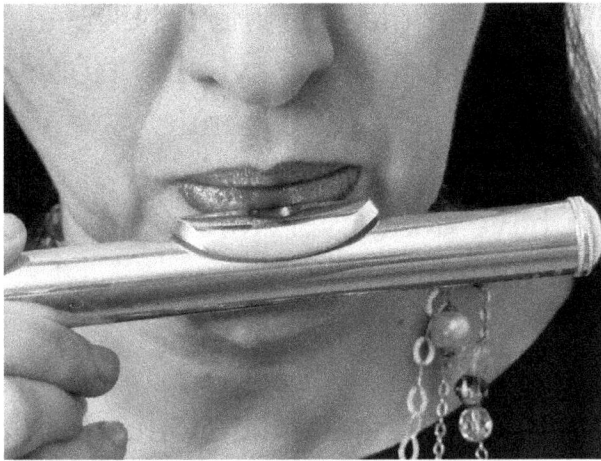

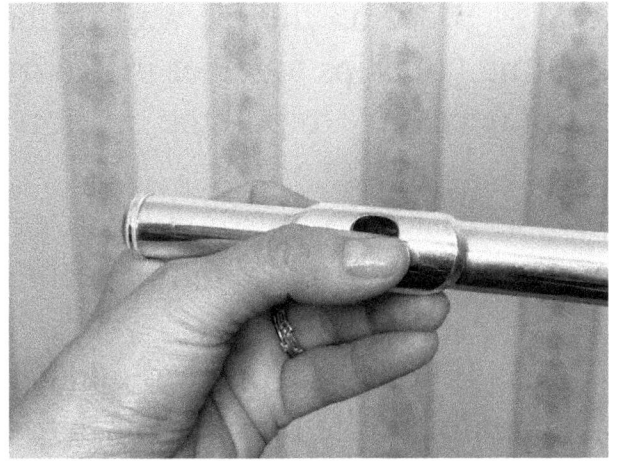

Incorrect positioning of the flute head joint on the lips:

Directing the Air Into the Flute Head

You should not blow directly inside the embouchure hole in the lip plate. Instead, direct the flow toward the far side of the riser. The airflow hits the wall of the riser, then curls and spirals into the flute's channel, changing its length as the keys open and close. This is how the sound on the flute is created. To help you make your first sound on the head joint, I have broken it down into a few steps:

1. Tense your abdominal muscles and take a deep breath into your lungs while keeping your shoulders down.

2. Right after you take deep breath, close your lips for a second and hold your breath. This allows you to exhale slowly and evenly later. Keep your abs tense and keep them tense during the whole time of directing air into the flute.

3. Blow on the far wall of the riser in the lip plate of the flute head joint. Bring your lips together in a narrow tube and visualize the syllable "fooh". It is not necessary to pull the lips forward or stretch them into a smile.

4. Listen to the sound you get: if you have done everything correctly, you should hear a sound reminiscent of a toy train whistle.

5. If you hear something like hissing and you don't get a good sound, breathe in again. While blowing air onto the far wall of the riser, change the position of the embouchure hole in the flute lip plate just a little by gently turning it toward you and then gently turning it away from you. This way the air will hit different parts of the riser. At some point the position will be right and the sound will appear. It may take some time, but you will succeed. The main thing is determination and perseverance.

6. When you have learned to produce the sound, you need to continue to strengthen it. Inhale and exhale the sound for 4–6 seconds to begin with. Then increase the length of exhalation up to 6–10 seconds. This is necessary for the uninterrupted playing of long musical phrases in flute pieces.

Producing the sound on the flute head joint

7. Further on, at the beginning of each exhalation use the tongue to articulate the beginning of the sound. Imagine as if you were getting ready to say "tew", but without saying it. All you need to do is blow. You will get a clearer beginning of the sound at the beginning of the exhalation called an "*attack*". Playing with such an attack is called *détaché*. You will start your lessons by using this particular articulation technique.

Remember that the task of blowing the sound on the flute head joint is to find a stable, correct position of the lip plate of the flute head on your lower lip. Try to achieve an even, long-lasting sound (without taking frequent breaths), take breaks for 1–2 minutes if the muscles of your face and lips get tired. You should get used to it and feel how the sound is created! While playing, keep your larynx as open as possible, like when yawning. If you feel dizzy due to hyperventilation, you may want to pause for a while.

5. Playing Posture

Playing Posture of the Body, Head, Hands, and Fingers on the Instrument; Embouchure; Tonguing and Breathing

In this section, we will look at the body position, the way you hold the instrument, the character of your playing movements, and how to make sound when playing the transverse flute. The main goal is to find the most comfortable position to avoid unnecessary tension and to play freely and easily with minimal energy expenditure.

Keep your body straight and natural, feet shoulder width apart, shoulders slightly turned and elbows slightly raised, not touching the sides of the body, so that the chest is not compressed and breathing is free. Keep your head straight without tilting, your face neither up nor down. It is best to control all these positions by looking at yourself in the mirror. Take the fully assembled flute in your hands. Hold the flute horizontally without lowering its right side. The hands will be positioned exactly as in the picture: the left hand is placed edgeways and closer to the head joint. The right hand is turned palm down and close to the foot joint of the flute. Avoid excessive bending of the hands at the wrists — the wrist should form a straight line with the forearm.

To maintain balance, the flute rests on three points of support:

1) The base of the first phalanx of the index finger of the left hand. We place the flute on it with the lower part of the body near the lower keys.

2) The lower jaw, including a part of the lower lip.

3) The thumb of the right hand — supporting the body of the flute from below.

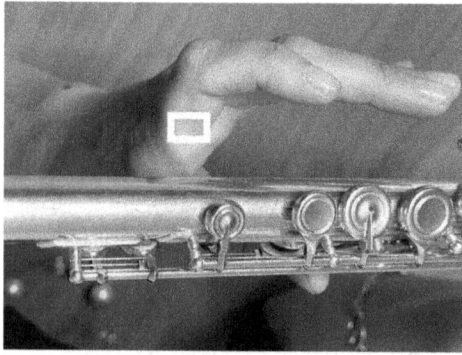

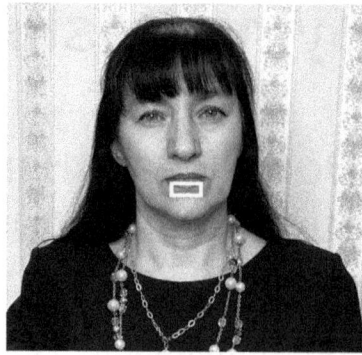

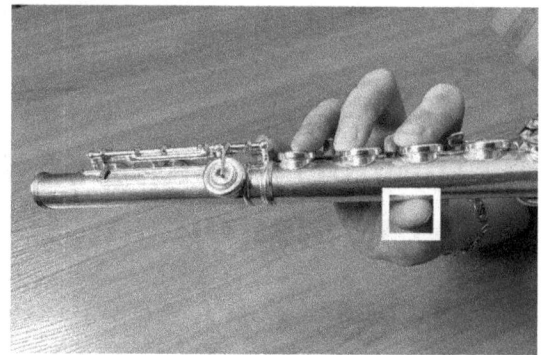

| Point 1 | Point 2 | Point 3 |

All three support points work to hold the instrument while playing — the left hand supports the flute from below, the place under the lower lip resists the pressure of the left hand, and the flute rests on the thumb of the right hand with its center point. This way the flute has a stable position in which the flutist's lips and fingers remain free and able to play the flute.

Never place the weight of the instrument in the curve between the index finger and thumb of the left hand — this will make it difficult for the fingers to move. Also, the flute should never move to the base of the thumb of the right hand. This is not an effective flute playing position. It may be uncomfortable to hold the flute for the first time. The flute may try to fall out of your hands, but please be patient and sensible and it will all come together.

☑

Do not turn your head toward your left shoulder and rest the flute on it. This is a wrong position that will not help create good sound. Instead, to bring the flute head joint and lip plate into the playing position, you should move your hands with the flute so far to the right that the flute lip plate is right at the center of your lips. Also, do not move your right arm back, lower it, or rest your right el-bow on your side. This will inevitably affect the flute's horizontal position and also the sound production.

Finger Placement and Function

All fingers that press the keys must remain free to drop and lift quickly. Pay attention to the fingers: they should not be tense, straight like pencils, or bent like hammers.

The order of the fingers on the keys of a musical instrument is called fingering. You will learn the entire flute fingering on pages 83–85 (see page 86 for a printout). For now, we'll only discuss the starting position of the fingers. This is the preparatory position before pressing the keys. The fingers are placed on the primary keys (1–9) about half an inch from the surface or resting on them without actually pressing the keys.

$\longrightarrow$

Now let's list the names of the flute keys and levers:

The positioning of the fingers of the left hand on the flute:

1. The thumb is placed on the lower key of B (1) or B-flat (1a). The finger moves freely during playing. Do not use it as a flute support!

2. The index finger is placed on the C (2) key.

3. The middle finger is placed on the A key (3).

4. The ring finger is placed on the G key (4).

5. The little finger rests on the G-sharp lever (5).

The word "rests" here refers only to the place for the finger. Whether the key (lever) is pressed or released will be shown when you learn the notes.

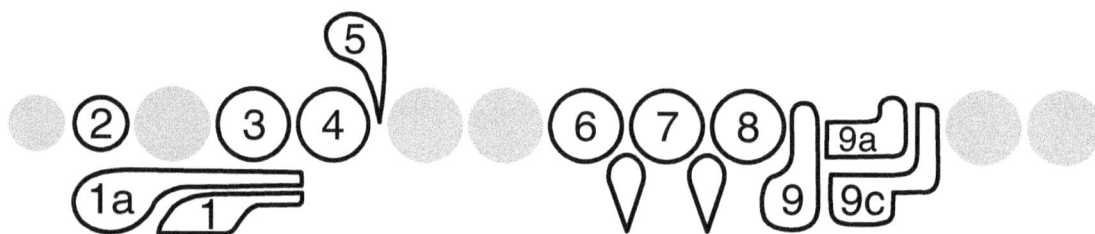

The position of the fingers of the right hand:

1. The thumb is used to support the flute. It is not involved in producing sound. Place your thumb under the body of the flute from below exactly opposite your index finger. Make sure that the muscles in your right wrist do not get tight.

2. Place your index finger on the F key (6).

3. The middle finger is placed on the E key (7).

4. The ring finger is located on the D key (8).

5. The little finger is placed primarily on the auxiliary lever (9), shifting to the right on the notes C and C-sharp (9a, 9c). The little finger must almost constantly press on the auxiliary lever (9) because the key it controls must be open at all times. The exceptions are the D notes of the fourth and fifth octaves and the C of the seventh octave.

The fingers of the hand should be slightly rounded, as if you were holding a small apple, not straight. Avoid "bending back" the fingers of the first phalanx, as this contributes to excessive muscle tension and negatively affects the mobility and rhythmic movements of the fingers. Pay special attention to the little finger of the right hand, which constantly presses the lever (9) — it should be

30

rounded, not straight, otherwise the wrist of the right hand may also get tense.

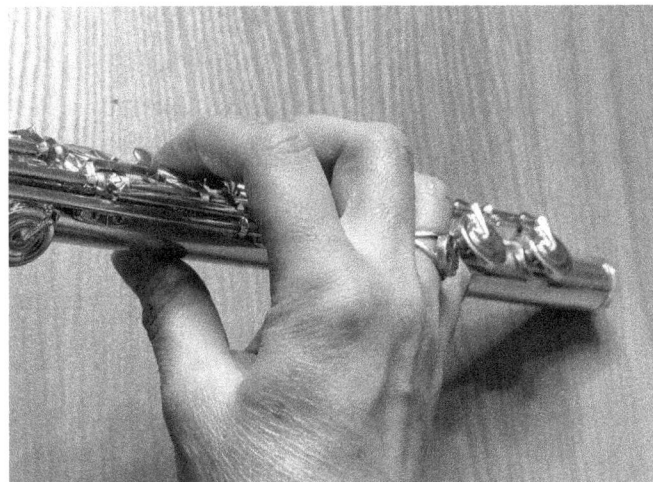

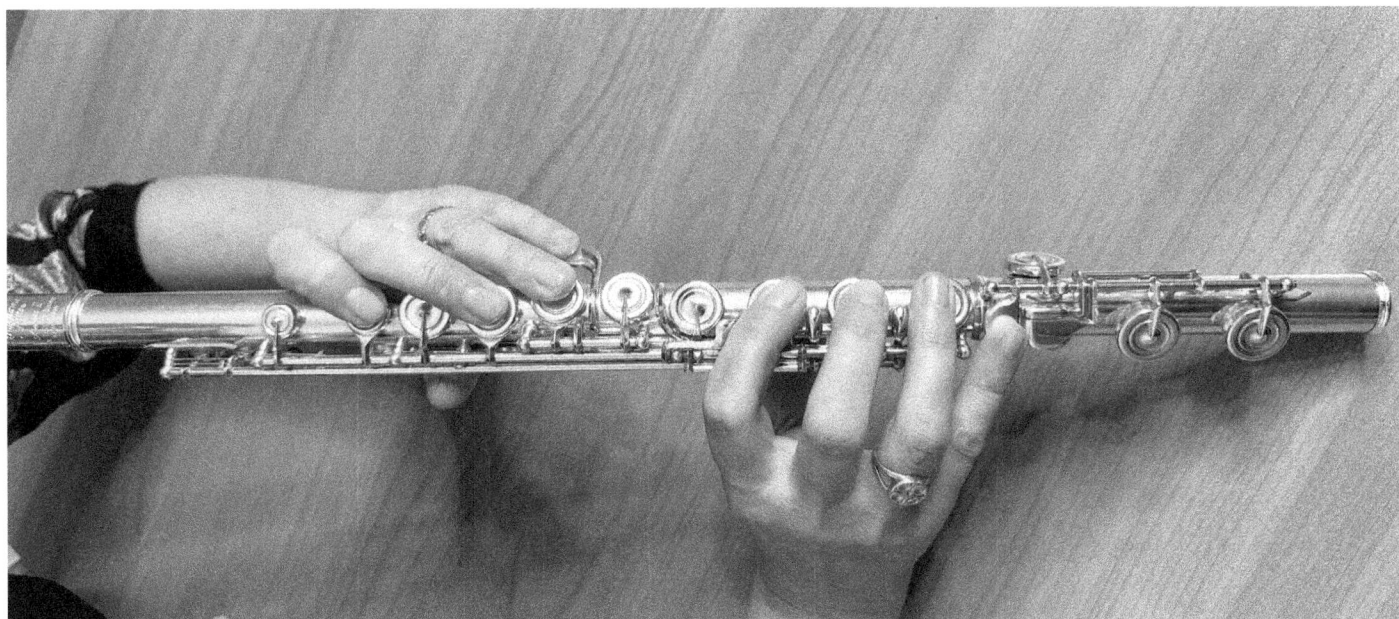

You're just about ready to start playing separate notes on the flute and mastering beginning music theory and simple pieces — all that waiting for you in Part 2.

Finger positioning on the keys

But wait!

There are two more interesting points you should know about in advance.

Point #1. Flutists do not look at their fingers while playing as if they were blindfolded. You will need to learn to feel each of your fingers and control the movements of your fingers one at a time and the movements of several fingers at once. While playing the piano requires one finger to press a single key to play a single note, playing the flute requires several fingers to press a combination of several keys at the same time to play a single note. The fingers do not always move together as they please. Often when alternating notes you have to raise one finger and at the same time lower the other. Therefore, pay attention when studying the fingering and do not rush. Learn one note properly before moving on to study the next one.

Point #2. The pitch of the sound on the flute depends on the length of the flute channel. This means that to move from high to low sounds in the fourth octave range, we close gradually and alternately all the keys on the flute from left to right. However, to make the sounds of the fifth and sixth octaves, the player must master a technique called "octave blowing." In the fourth and fifth octaves many notes have the same fingering (position of the fingers on the keys), but the force of air blowing into the flute barrel must be greater and the lip opening must be smaller. The air flow into the flute channel should be even greater when playing in the sixth octave, but there the fingering of each note has its own peculiarities, which you can study in the fingering diagrams.

The process of octave blowing

Playing in Different Positions

You can play sitting, standing (even walking, such as in a band), but it is easier for beginners to master the instrument standing up. Solo flutists usually play on stage standing up.

Sitting down is easier because you do not get as tired and can spend more time practicing. If you sometimes want to play sitting down, you should sit on the front edge of a chair, lean on your feet, and sit with a straight back. Avoid comfortable chairs with armrests, as it is difficult to maintain proper posture in them. Get a stiffer chair, such as a kitchen chair. Never recline on the backrest

if the chair has one. You should be sitting straight up. Your legs should neither be tucked under you nor stretched forward. Knees should be bent at a 90 degree angle.

What Else You Need to Know to Play Using Sheet Music

Detaché (detached) means playing individual notes on the flute that do not have any additional markings above them. When you make the sound from the flute head joint and on a fully assembled flute, you simply blow into it, representing the syllable "few". The tongue does not take part in this process. When performing using sheet music, it is customary to make the beginning of the sound clearer by means of the sound "attack". That is the movement of the tongue that is reminiscent of the syllable "tew": the tongue touches the upper palate and the back of the teeth, just as when pronouncing the "t" sound, but it should not stick out between the lips. It is important to realize that the tongue does not create the sound. It only blocks the exit of the air pressure directed into the instrument.

Legato (slurred) means connecting notes together on a continuous exhalation of air. It is indicated in the sheet music by a curved line above the notes, called *a slur.* If you see that such an arc is drawn from one note through several others, then you should start the first note by attacking the sound with your tongue, and then continue to blow air into the flute, and with your fingers press the necessary keys to play the notes — the melody will sound smoothly, and one sound will flow smoothly into another. However, in this case, you should

33

pay attention to the coordination of the work of the fingers, so that the movements are nimble and the fingers are raised in time. Otherwise, the transition from one note to the next will not happen accurately.

Staccato (sharply detached) — a technique for playing a short sound (about half of the written duration), indicated by dots above or below the note. You can shorten the sound by stopping the exhalation, or you can close the air outlet with your tongue, like when saying the syllable "tute". The movement of the tongue should be coordinated in time with the movements of the fingers and supported by a strong rush of exhalation.

Ending the sound — there is a soft and a hard way to end the sound. Soft ending or tapering of the sound is performed without the tongue, only by decreasing and stopping the breath. Hard ending is done using the tongue, which acts as a valve used to shut off air to the embouchure opening in the lip plate.

Tuning Your Flute

The flute does not have a fixed pitch, so it must be tuned every time before playing with the piano, in an ensemble with other instruments, or to an accompaniment track.

To tune the flute, it is more convenient to use a tuner — a device that indicates the correct pitch of the sound. As a rule, the tuner has a frequency of vibration of the A of the fourth octave which equals 440 Hz. This sound serves as the starting point of tuning for all acoustic instruments. Those who want to perform authentic early music, set the fourth octave A note vibration frequency slightly lower, to 432 Hz. There is an app "Tuner and Metronome" ("Tuner by Piascore") that can be installed on a cell phone, tablet or computer.

The flute is adjusted to the desired frequency pattern by sliding the flute head joint in or out of the main body of the flute. Start by playing the A note and look at the tuner to see if the indicator arrow falls within the range of the right pitch. If the indicator goes up beyond that range, then you should pull the flute head out of the body just a little, about 1–2 millimeters and play again while looking at the tuner. If the flute's pitch is lower, push the head joint inside the body just a little bit, and check the tuner. The tuning capacity is built-in by the manufacturers, so if you initially push the flute head into the body as far as it will go, the sound will be high relative to the standard.

However, you should be aware that the note will not always correspond exactly to the tuner's reading. In this case, there is a method of more precise tuning — it is adjusting the position of the hole in the flute's lip plate in relation to the airflow. If you want to raise the pitch, you slightly turn the embouchure hole away from you. And the opposite is true: turn it toward you if the pitch needs to be lowered.

Tuning the flute using a tuner

Producing Sound, Basic Errors and Troubleshooting Tips

Take note: using improper technique, faulty breathing and incorrect hand placement when working on your tone and finger coordination can make you ineffective, cause fatigue and reinforce the mistakes, which will not be easy to get rid of later.

If you blow too hard, you will produce a harsh, whistling, unpleasant sound. Try blowing softer to create a more melodic sound. Depending on the melody, the airflow can be faster or slower, but exhalation should always be supported by tense abdominal muscles.

An important point: don't puff up your cheeks or raise your shoulders when you take a breath. These things can easily become bad habits and also make it difficult to maintain an even tone. Check visually by looking in the mirror — how you breathe in and breathe out. Take a breath — do your shoulders go up? If they do, then you need to fix your breathing. Breathe out. Tense your abs again and inhale as if you were smelling your favorite fragrance — your stomach and rib cage should expand, but your shoulders and chest should remain in place. You got it!

PART 2

Theory and Practice

All Videos (Playlist)

All videos are included in the same playlist on YouTube *(online):*

or use the link:

cutt.ly/Krm3nGc8

All Audios and PDF Files for Downloading

All of the audio ▶ and PDF files are also available on Google Drive:

or use the link:

cutt.ly/6rmHXxI2

1. Important! Be sure to download all files from Google Drive to your computer. We did have a glitch in our system once and our files were temporarily unavailable online. It would be best to download them all at once so you have offline access to them anytime.

2. In songs with accompaniment in audio files marked with "+" sign you will hear an example of how to play the melody (flute plays the melody and flute plays solo). The audio files marked with "-" have no melody, just the accompaniment track. It is there for you to play along with.

For any questions, comments or suggestions, email us at:
avgustaudartseva@gmail.com

Introduction

It is certainly not enough to know how to press the keys on the flute. Likewise, it is important to understand and read written music. To achieve this, you need to acquire musical literacy, which is not that difficult. After learning the basic theory, you can use it to play not just the flute, but literally any other instrument!

The world of music will be open to you, and you will be able to read melodies that are familiar to you and that you like.

Not only will your repertoire increase, but you will also be able to record your own music, should you come up with a unique melody in a moment of inspiration.

This book contains different songs and melodies that are easy to play. Some songs have lyrics making it easier to understand the structure of musical phrases and help you play more expressively.

1. The Stave, Notes and Treble Clef

Music is written on a set of 5 lines called **a stave** (staff[1]). The two clefs that are most commonly used are **the treble clef** and **the bass clef.**

Music notes are oval-shaped symbols that are placed on the lines or in spaces between them. They represent musical sounds called **pitches.**

The lines of the stave are numbered from bottom to top (1–5). The spaces between the lines are also numbered from bottom to top (1–4). If the notes appear higher on the stave, they sound higher in pitch. If the notes appear lower on the stave, they sound lower in pitch.

The Treble Clef

The Stave (Staff)

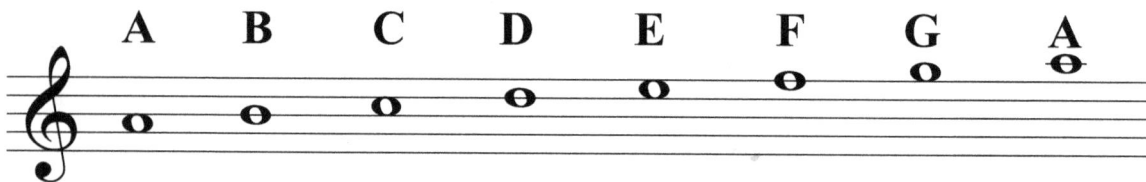

Music notes are named after the first seven letters of the alphabet:
A, B, C, D, E, F, G.

---

[1]Staff and stave have the same meaning: 'staff' is more commonly used in American English, while 'stave' is preferred in British English. For the purposes of this book, we will use 'stave.'

In the treble clef the names of the notes on the lines from bottom to top are **E, G, B, D, F.**

Notes on the Line

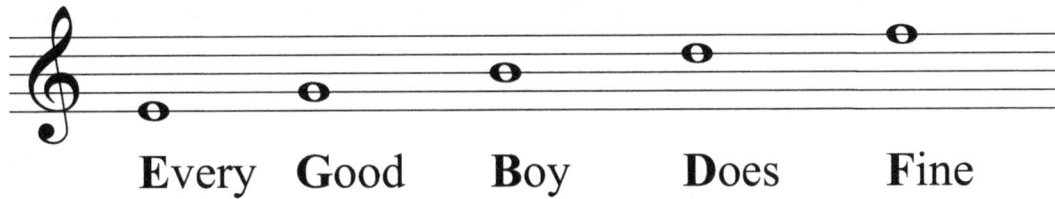

Every   Good   Boy   Does   Fine

Notes in the Spaces

The names of the notes in the spaces from bottom to top spell **FACE.**

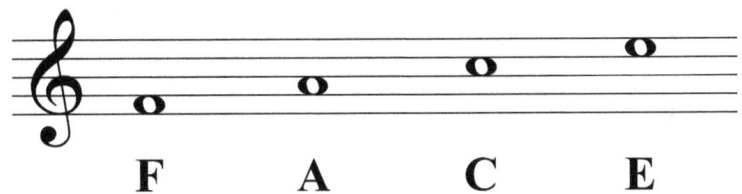

F   A   C   E

Ledger lines are those little lines with notes on them that appear above or below a musical stave.

The purpose of these lines is to extend the stave in both directions, up and down.

An octave is simply the distance between one note and that same note repeated in the next higher or lower register within the audible range.

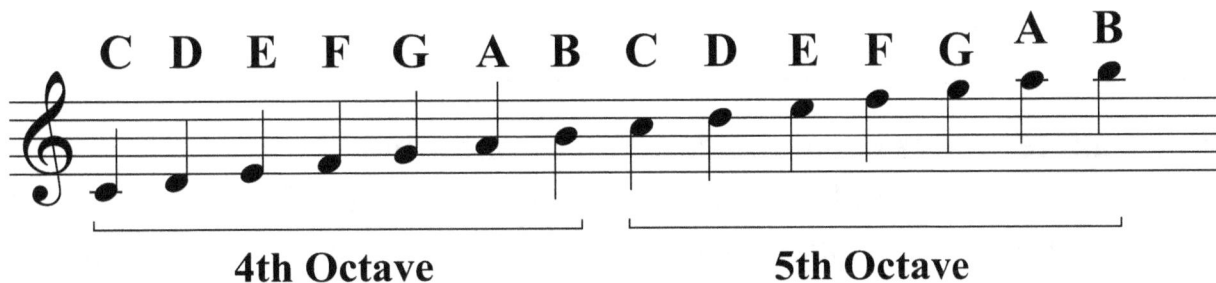

4th Octave   **5th Octave**

You can see that the notes are repeated (and there are 7 of them in total). The same note played an octave up sounds exactly the same, just higher.

Stems extend downward on the left side when the note appears on or above the 3rd line of the stave. Stems extend upward on the right side when the note appears below the 3rd line of the stave.

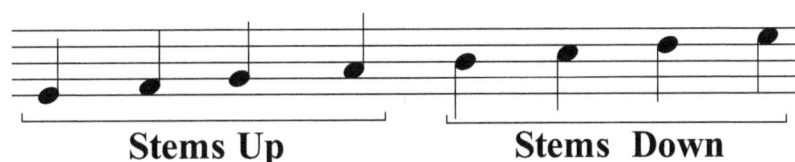

Stems Up   **Stems Down**

41

2. Note Values

While the placement of notes on the stave indicates the pitch, the duration of the note (how long the note is held down) is determined by the value of the note.

A whole note is drawn as an open oval.

A whole note is equal to four counts (or beats). Count and clap the rhythm evenly (hands together for 4 beats). The beat numbers are written under the notes. Also, say "ta-ah-ah-ah" (in a continuous sound) and clap.

Whole note

o = 4 beats

(1 and 2 and 3 and 4 and)

1 2 3 4

ta -ah -ah -ah

Two half notes equal the duration of one whole note.

A half note is equal to two counts (or beats). Count and clap the rhythm evenly (hold your hands together for 2 beats). The beat numbers are written under the notes. Also, say "ta-ah" (in a continuous sound) and clap.

Half notes

= 2 beats

(1 and 2 and)

1 2   3 4

ta -ah   ta -ah

Four quarter notes equal the duration of one whole note.

A quarter note is equal to one count (or beat). Count (1, 2, 3, 4) and clap the rhythm evenly (once per beat). The beat numbers are written under the notes. Also, say "ta" and clap.

Quarter notes

= 1 beat (1 and)

1   2   3   4

ta ta ta ta

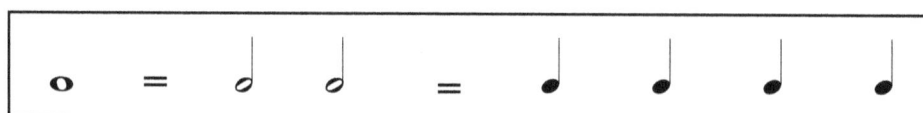

3. $\frac{4}{4}$ Time Signature, Measure, Bar Line

The time signature appears at the beginning of the music after the clef sign. It contains two numbers, one above the other.

The upper number indicates how many beats (or counts) are in each measure. In this case, there are 4.

The lower number indicates what type of note receives 1 beat. In this case, it's a quarter note.

The two numbers in the time signature are often replaced by the letter **C**.

$$\frac{4}{4} = \mathbf{C}$$

Music is divided into equal parts by **bar lines.** The area between the two bar lines is called **a measure** or **bar.**

The end bar line is written at the end of a piece of music. It is made up of one thin and one thick line, with the thick line always on the outside.

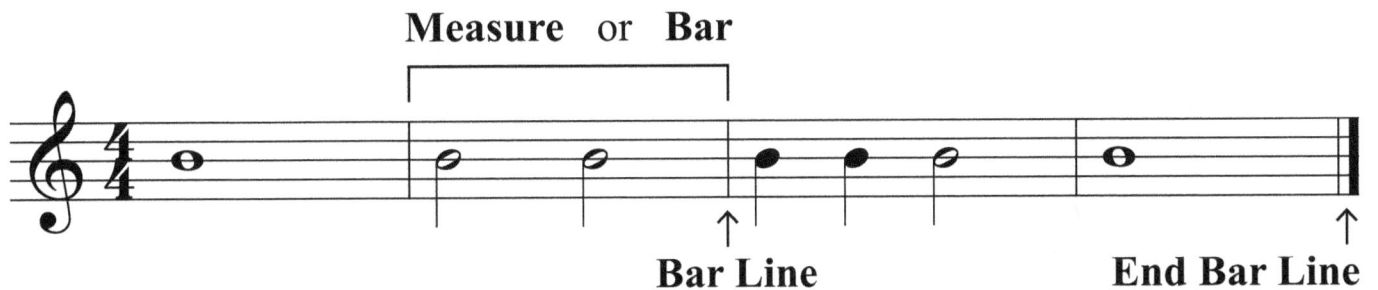

Measure or Bar

Bar Line

End Bar Line

The Note B

Watch the video

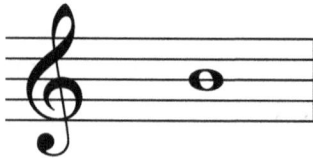

Practice the Long Tones

It is important to practice playing the **long notes.** These are notes played for as long as you exhale. The long note exercise is practiced at the beginning of every flute lesson.

Play B ——————————— Take a breath ——————————— Etc.

1 *Air attack*   **Tie**   *Air attack*

    1 2 3 4   1 2 3 4   1 2 3 4   1 2 3 4

A tie joins two notes of the same pitch by a curved line over or under the notes. Each note joined by a tie is held for its full value, but only the first note is played or sung. The tied note's value is added to the value of the first note.

2 *Tongue attack*

too   too too   too too too   too
1 2 3 4 1 2 3 4 1 2 3 4 1 2 3 4

Page 44

3 *Tongue attack*

too too too too   too too too too   too too too too

4. Rests

Music is not only made up of sounds, but also the silence between sounds. The duration of musical silence is determined by the value of **the rest.**

A whole rest means to rest for a whole measure. It hangs down from the 4th line.	
A half rest is equal to half of a whole rest. It sits on the 3rd line.	
A quarter rest is equal to one quarter of a whole rest.	

In the 4/4 time:

The quarter rest is equal to 1 beat.	
The half rest is equal to 2 beats.	
The whole rest is equal to 4 beats.	

1 quarter note = 1 beat   1 quarter rest = 1 silent beat

Clap the rhythm while counting

The Note A

Pages 46–49

1 ▶ ↓ *Air attack* *Stop air* Half rest ↓ *Tongue attack* *Stop with tongue* ↓

1 2 3 4   1 2 3 4   1 2 3 4   1 2 3 4

Repeat signs enclose a passage that is to be played twice.

Play long notes while gradually increasing volume on the first note and gradually decreasing volume on the second note.

Ending long notes is usually done without the help of the tongue, which gives a gradual fading of the sound.

Often there are indications above the notes in the form of a V or a comma, which denote where you may take a breath.

2 ▶

B   V A

Symbol	Italian	English
<	*crescendo*	Gradually get louder
>	*diminuendo*	Gradually get softer

3 ▶ ↓ *Tongue attack*

too　too　　too　too　too　too　too　too　too　too

1　2　3　4　　1　2　3　4　　1　2　3　4　　1　2　3　4

too　　too　　too　too　　too　　　　too　too

1　2　3　4　　1　2　3　4　　1　2　3　4　　1　2　3　4

4 ▶

A　A　B　　A　A　B　B　VA　A　B　　A　B　　A V

1　2　3　4　　1　2　3　4　　1　2　3　4　　1　2　3　4

B　　A　　A　B　B　　VB　　A　　A

1　2　3　4　　1　2　3　4　　1　2　3　4　　1　2　3　4

5. Eighth Note

When you add a flag to the stem of a quarter note, it becomes **an eighth note.**

Stem → (Flag, Note head)

Two eighth notes equal the duration of one quarter note. An eighth note is equal to a half of a count (or beat).

Eighth notes

♪ ♪ = 1 beat = ♩
1 and

♪ = 1/2 beat

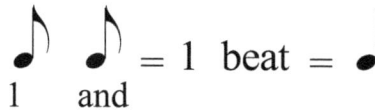

Count (1 and 2 and 3 and 4 and) and clap the rhythm evenly (once per beat and once per "and"). The beat numbers are written under the notes. Also, say "tee" and clap.

1	and	2	and	3	and	4	and
tee	tee	tee	tee	tee	tee	tee	tee

Two or more 8th notes are connected by a beam.

Beam

♫ ♫ or ♫♫

Two eighth notes equal 1 quarter note	♪ ♪ = ♩ = **1 beat**
	1 and tee tee
Four eighth notes equal 1 half note	♫♫ = ♩ = **2 beats**
	1 and 2 and tee tee tee tee
Eight eighth notes equal 1 whole note	♫♫♫♫ = o = **4 beats**
	1 and 2 and 3 and 4 and tee tee tee tee tee tee tee tee

Clap the rhythm while counting

The whole note   The half notes   The quarter notes   The eighth notes

1   2   3   4   1   2   3   4   1   2   3   4   1 and 2 and 3 and 4 and

ta -ah-ah-ah   ta -ah   ta -ah   ta   ta   ta   ta   tee tee tee tee   tee tee tee tee

5 ▶

A A B   A B A   B B B B A   ⋁B   A A   B B B A   ⋁

1 & 2 & 3 & 4 &   1 & 2 & 3 & 4 &   1 & 2 & 3 & 4 &   1 & 2 & 3 & 4 &

B B A   A B A B A   ⋁B   A B   A   A

1 & 2 & 3 & 4 &   1 & 2 & 3 & 4 &   1 & 2 & 3 & 4 &   1 & 2 & 3 & 4 &

The Note G

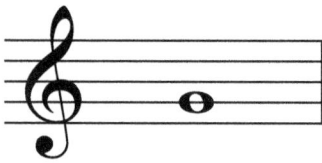

Pages 50–51

Practice the long tone

1 ▶
G   ∨G   ∨A   ∨B

2 ▶

too   too   too   too   too   too   too   too   too   too   too
1   2   3   4   1   2   3   4   1   2   3   4   1   2   3   4

Clap the rhythm while counting

1 & 2 & 3 & 4 &   1 & 2 & 3 & 4 &   1 & 2 & 3   & 4 &   1 & 2 & 3 & 4 &

3 ▶
G   G   A   A A   B   B   ∨A A A G   A   A   B   A   G   ∨

1   2   3   4   1 & 2   3   4   1 & 2 & 3   4   1   2   3   4

G   A   B B B B B   A   ∨A A A A A   G   G

1   2   3   4   1 & 2 & 3   4   1 & 2 & 3   4   1   2   3   4

Now you can play these songs:

Hot Cross Buns ▶

Hot cross buns! Hot cross buns!   One a pen-ny, two a pen-ny, hot cross buns!

Down by the Station ▶

Down   by   the   sta - tion   ear - ly   in   the   morn - ing,

Down   by   the   sta - tion   hear   the   whis - tle   blow.

Sleep, Baby, Sleep ▶

Traditional

Sleep,   ba - by   sleep,   The   fath - er   tends   the   sheep.

Moth - er   shakes   the   dream-land   tree,   And   down   fall   pleas - ant

dreams   for   thee,   Sleep,   ba - by,   sleep.

6. $\frac{2}{4}$ and $\frac{3}{4}$ Time Signatures

$\frac{2}{4}$ 2 means that there are 2 beats per measure;
4 means that the quarter note receives 1 beat.

$\frac{2}{4}$ and $\frac{4}{4}$ both have 4 as the bottom number, meaning a quarter note receives 1 beat. The difference is that $\frac{2}{4}$ has 2 beats per measure, while $\frac{4}{4}$ has 4.

A whole rest is used for a full measure of rest even if there are only 2 beats in each measure. When writing music, a half rest and a whole note are never used in $\frac{2}{4}$ time.

$\frac{3}{4}$ 3 means that there are 3 beats per measure;
4 means that the quarter note receives 1 beat.

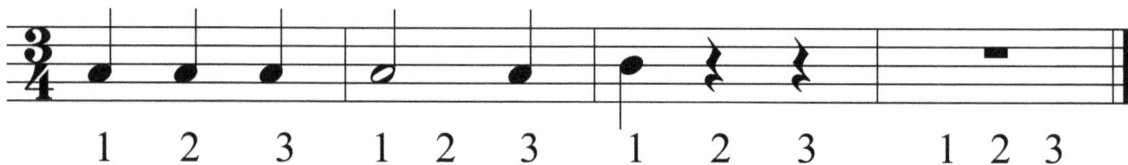

A whole rest is used for a full measure of rest even if there are only 3 beats in each measure. When writing the music, a half rest and a whole note are never used in $\frac{3}{4}$ time.

$\frac{2}{4}$, $\frac{3}{4}$ and $\frac{4}{4}$ all have 4 as the bottom number, meaning the quarter note always receives 1 beat.

The Note C

Page 53

Practice the long tone

Play C ▶

too   too   too   too   too   too   too too too
1   2   3   4   1   2   3   4   1   2   3   4   1   &   2   3   4

Barcarolle ▶

Jacques Offenbach

1   2   3   1   2   3   1   2   3   1   2   3

1   2   3   1   2   3   1   2   3   1   2   3

The Joke ▶

Natalia Tolbatova

The Note D

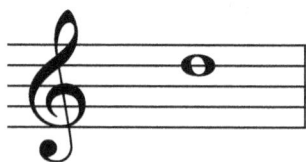 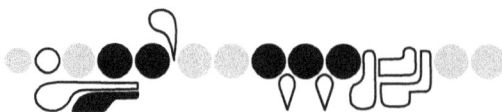 

Pages 54–55

Practice the long tone

To be able to play the notes in the fifth and sixth octaves, the player must master a technique called "octave blowing" — the force of air blowing into the embouchure hole of the flute barrel must be slightly greater than when playing the previous notes. Also, the opening between the lips must be slightly smaller.

Play D ▶

too   too   too   too   too   too   too   too   too
1   2   3   4   1   2   3   4   1   2   3   4   1   2   3   4

God Is So Good ▶

God   is   so   good,   God   is   so   good,

God   is   so   good,   He's   so   good   to   me.

54

Ode to Joy ▶

Ludwig van Beethoven

Remember

55

The Note F

Page 56

Practice the long tone

Play F ▶

too   too too too   too   too too too too   too too   too too too

Mary Had a Little Lamb ▶

Sarah Josepha Hale
1866

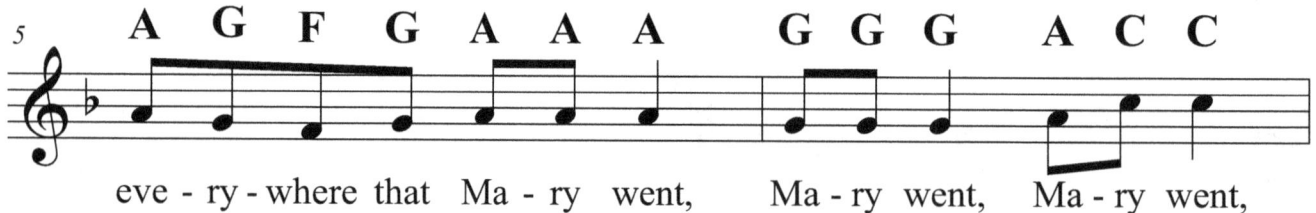

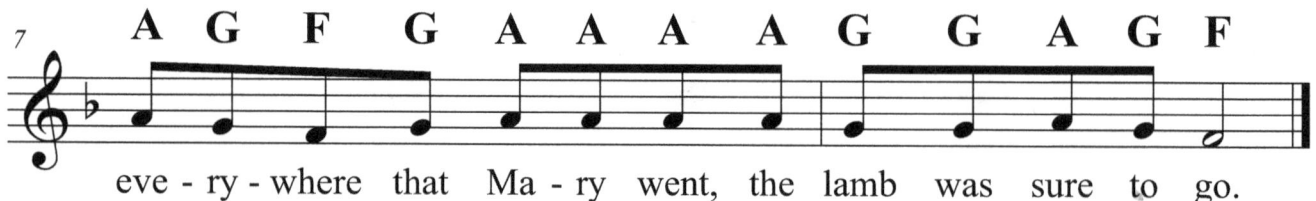

How to Play Lower Notes

1. Check the tension of the abdominal abs — this is the key to quality exhalation.
2. Use your lips to direct the airflow downwards, towards the floor. The speed of the air flow should be slightly reduced, blowing more quietly and precisely on the riser.
3. To master a good tone, start with a higher note, where you feel more comfortable, and then work your way down successively to the note you want to learn.
4. Learn the fingering in advance to make pressing the keys correctly easier.

The Note E

Page 57

Practice the long tone

Play E ▶

too   too   too   too   too   too   too   too

1 & 2 & 1 & 2 & 1 & 2 & 1 & 2 &

Lucy Locket ▶

G G A A G G E E G G A A G E ∨

Lu - cy Lock - et   lost her pock - et,   Kit - ty Fish - er   found it.

G G A A G G E E G G A A G E

Not a pen - ny   was there in   it,   on - ly rib - bon round it.

The Note D

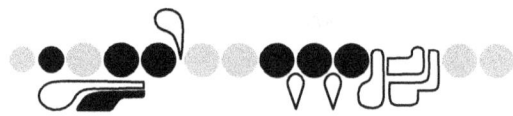

Page 58

D

Practice the long tone

The Trail

Natalia Tolbatova

The Note C

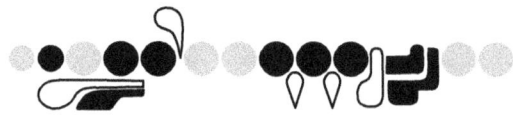

C

Practice the long tone

Little Boy

Natalia Tolbatova

C Major Scale

A scale is a set of notes that are ordered in pitch.

Now you know how to play the basic notes, and this sequence forms the C major scale.

Play each note at a slow tempo starting with the bottom C.

If you still have difficulty playing the low notes of the C major scale, try to play it in reverse order.

The fingering of these notes in the fifth octave is the same as the fingering of the same notes in the fourth octave, but you must use the octave overblowing method — the force of air blowing into the flute barrel channel must be greater, and the opening between your lips must be smaller. If necessary, go back to step 5 and rewatch the video of this process.

There are major and minor scales for all notes. On page 113, you will find a scale that is easy to learn.

7. Sharp, Flat and Enharmonic Notes

The sharp sign (♯) before a note raises the pitch of that note.

The flat sign (♭) before a note lowers the pitch of that note.

The note which is half a step higher than D is D-sharp. On the piano, this is the black key to the immediate right of D. The note which is half a step lower than E is E-flat. On the piano, this is the black key to the immediate left of E.

But isn't this the same key? Why do they have different names, you might ask. There's a term used to describe this and it's called enharmonics. D-sharp and E-flat are enharmonic equivalents because while they are played by the same key, they have different note names.

Enharmonic notes — two notes that sound the same but are written differently.

On the flute just as on the keyboard, one combination of closed holes can be written in two ways (a note with a flat or a note with a sharp). Here are the five basic pairs.

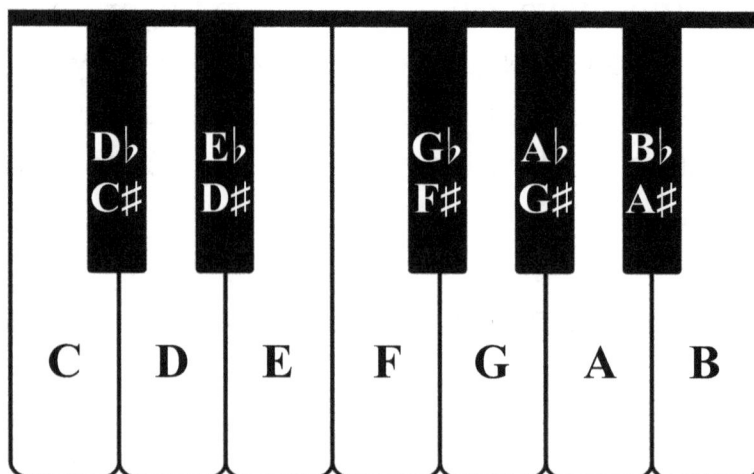

There's D-flat (or C-sharp), E-flat (or D-sharp), G-flat (or F-sharp), A-flat (or G-sharp) and B-flat (or A-sharp).

8. Key Signatures

Usually certain sharps or flats are used throughout the piece. Writing in those sharps or flats every time they appear takes time and adds clutter. Instead, composers put them in a key signature found just after the clef at the beginning of each stave. Key signatures tell us what notes are always sharp or flat in a given piece of music. Always read the sharps or flats in a key signature. Key signatures always have the sharps and flats listed in the same order. They always follow the same pattern.

The Sharps #

The Flats ♭

Natural ♮

♮ This sign overrides all previous signs (flats or sharps) in a measure.

See also page 111.

The Note F#

Pages 62–66

Rain, Rain, Go Away

| A | F# | A A F# | A A F# B | A A F# |

Rain, rain, go a - way, come a - gain a - noth - er day.

| G G E E | G G E | A G F# E | F# D D |

Lit - tle child - ren want to play, Rain___ Rain___ go a - way.

London Bridge Is Falling Down

| A B A G | F# G A | E F# G | F# G A |

Lon - don Bridge is fall - ing down, fall - ing down, fall - ing down,

| A B A G | F# G A | E A | F# D |

Lon - don Bridge is fall - ing down, My fair la - dy.

Each note joined by a tie is held for its full value, but only the first note is played. The tied note's value is added to the value of the first note.

Tie

1 2 3 4 1 2 3 & 4

62

9. Articulation

Articulation is the manner in which a note is performed.

Non legato — the sounds are pronounced separately using the tongue. The duration of the note is fully sustained.

[1] ▶ Play the G major scale. All tongued

G   A   B   C   D   E   F♯   G   F♯   E   D   C   B   A   G

A slur smoothly connects two or more notes of different pitches by a curved line over or under the notes. There is no break in sound between pitches. This is also called playing or singing *legato* — a smooth connection of sounds without using the tongue.

[2] ▶ **Slur**   All slurred

Legato ▶

Natalia Tolbatova

Melody ▶

A. G. Rubinstein

Moderato

V

mp ——————— *mf*

V

mp

V

f

Tie

Tongue stop

Dots placed above or below note heads indicate that the notes should be played **staccato,** in a detached manner. Musicians often play a staccato quarter note as if it were an eighth note followed by an eighth rest. Short sound with a firm attack and a clear ending with the tongue, from Italian "*staccato*" — torn off, separated.

Golden Sun ▶

| C | B | | A | G | | F# | A | | G | E | | E |

| G | | F | D | | D | F | | E | C |

Held for full duration

Tenuto — the duration of the note is fully sustained. Sounds are extracted similarly to *non legato*, but more connected, gently separating each note with the tongue.

64

>
Accent — accented, emphatically firm attack of sound, duration is not shortened.

Heavy Accent,
play full length

Little Waltz ▶

Natalia Tolbatova

Allegretto

^

Marcato (accented, emphasized hard attack of sound, from the Italian "*marcato*" — marked).

A sharper, shorter and firmer accent, played as a bright staccato.

Heavy staccato
accent, play short
(Tongue stop)

A fermata can be found above a note or a rest. It simply means holding out the note for as long as you want to. It is the composer's idea to hold it for some length of time. If you specify the sounding duration of a note under the fermata, then you can assume that the note (or rest) should be extended by its original value — that is, doubled in length. So, if it's a half note, then it sounds like a whole note. If it is a whole note, then it sounds like two whole notes, etc.

Early One Morning ▶

English folk song

Moderato

Ear - ly one mor - ning, just as the sun was ri - sing. I heard a maid

sing - ing in the val - ley be - low: "O don't de - ceive me! Oh, ne - ver

leave me! How could you use a poor mai - den so?"

Eighth Rest

An eighth rest 𝄾 is equal to half the value of a quarter rest 𝄽.

Two 8th rests equal 1 quarter rest.
1 and

Four 8th rests equal 1 half rest.
1 and 2 and

Eight 8th rests equal 1 whole rest.
1 and 2 and 3 and 4 and

Eighth rests **Eighth notes**

Clap and play

1 & 2 & 3 & 4 & 1 & 2 & 3 & 4 & 1 & 2 & 3 & 4 & 1 & 2 & 3 & 4 &

66

Sixteenth Note

Sixteenth note = 1/4 beat

1 and   2 and   3 and   4 and

$\downarrow$ = $\downarrow\downarrow$ = $\downarrow\downarrow\downarrow\downarrow$

1 and   1 and   1   and

Clap the rhythm while counting

1   & 2 & 3 & 4   &   1 & 2   & 3 & 4   &   1& 2& 3   &   4&   1& 2 & 3& 4&

A sixteenth rest is equal to half the value of an eighth rest

γ = γ γ ξ = γ γ = γ γ γ γ

Clap the rhythm while counting

1   & 2 & 3& 4   &   1 & 2 & 3 & 4   &   1& 2& 3   & 4& 1& 2 & 3& 4&

10. Dotted Note

A dot is placed after the note to indicate a change in the duration of a note. The dot adds half of the value of the note to itself. For example, a dotted half note gets 3 beats — the value of a half note is 2, half of 2 is 1, so 2 + 1 = 3.

♩	+	♩	=	♩.		♩.	=	♩	♩	♩
2 beats		1 beat		3 beats		1 2 3		1	2	3

♩	+	♪	=	♩.		♩.	=	♪	♪	♪
1 beat		1/2 beat		1 and 2		1 and 2		1	and	2

| ♪ | + | ♬ | = | ♪. | | ♪. | = | ♬ | ♬ | ♬ |

Clap the rhythm while counting

1 & 2 & 3& 4 &   1& 2 &3& 4 &   1 &2 & 3 & 4&   1 & 2 & 3 & 4&

Dotted rhythms mix longer dotted notes with shorter undotted notes.

1 and   2 and   3 and   4 and   ♩. ♪ = ♩ = 1 beat

Clap the rhythm while counting

1 & 2 & 3 & 4 &   1 & 2 & 3& 4 &   1 & 2 & 3& 4& 1& 2& 3& 4&

Clap the rhythm while counting

1 & 2 &3 & 4& 1 &2 & 3 & 4 & 1 & 2 & 3 & 4& 1& 2& 3& 4&

68

11. 6/8 Time Signature

6
8
6 means that there are 6 beats per measure;
8 means that the eighth note receives 1 beat.

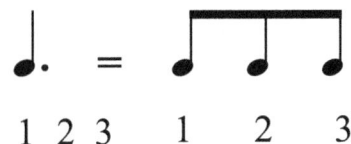

1 2 3   1   2   3

<u>How to count in 6/8 :</u>

There are two ways to count a bar in the 6/8 time. This can seem confusing when you first encounter it, but as you will see, the difference is not as big as it first appears.

You can either count it as:

- 6 eighth-note beats: 1, 2, 3, 4, 5, 6 = 1, 2, 3, 1, 2, 3
- 2 dotted-quarter-note beats: 1… 2…

Clap and say the beats

1 2 3   1 2 3   1 2 3 1 2 3   1 2 3   1 2 3

Play

Humpty Dumpty ▶

E   G F   A   G A B C

Hump - ty Dump - ty   sat   on   a   wall.

3 E   G F   A   G F E D

Hump - ty Dump - ty   had   a great fall.

Pages 69–70

12. Numbering of Measures

In this collection, the bars in each song are numbered. At the beginning of each next line of notes, a number is placed above the treble clef, which indicates the number of the measure.

The numbering of measures in the first note line is not indicated.

Play

Aura Lee ▶

music by George R. Poulton;
lyrics by W. W. Fosdick

As the black-bird in the spring 'neath the wil-low

→ 4 tree, Sat and piped I heard him sing

→ 7 prais-ing Au - ra Lee. Au - ra Lee!

→ 10 Au - ra Lee! Maid of gold - en hair.

→ 13 Sun - shine came a - long with thee and

→ 15 swal - lows in the air.

13. Incomplete Measure

A measure is a unit of music. It is the space (area of music) between two bar lines. The time signature (the 2 numbers at the beginning of the melody) indicates how many beats are in a measure.

A first measure is called **an incomplete measure** when it does not contain the full number of beats as indicated by the time signature.

The notes in the first incomplete measure (the part of the counts found at the beginning of the music) are called *the anacrusis,* pick-up or upbeat.

An incomplete measure is a measure that is split or divided between the beginning and the end of the music.

Part of the measure is found at the beginning of the music. The remaining part of the measure is found at the end of the music.

The two "parts" must add up to one complete (full) measure.

A-Tisket, A-Tasket

First incomplete measure

$\frac{4}{4}$ = 4 beats per measure.

Last incomplete measure

71

When a melody starts with an incomplete measure, it does not start with count #1!

Count #1 is the first count of the first complete measure. It is not necessarily the first count of the melody.

So, what is the first count of an incomplete measure? To figure this out, you must go to the end, to the last measure!

$\frac{3}{4}$ = 3 beats per measure.

Happy Birthday to You ▶

Pages 72–75

The beginning of the final measure will be count #1. So, start adding the counts there and, when you run out of beats, head back to the beginning and finish adding the counts.

The final measure will start with count #1. Start adding the counts there and when there are no more notes under which to write the counts, you have to go back to the beginning to finish the counting.

Why do we use an incomplete measure? Quite simply, it is all about the beat and the pulse. Try singing 'Happy Birthday' but start with a strong downbeat (strong pulse) instead of a weak upbeat (weak pulse). It just does not sound correct, does it?

The important tip to remember is that measure #1 is the first measure that has count #1! The first measure may not be measure #1. If there is no count #1 at the beginning of that measure, then it is an incomplete measure.

The anacrusis, upbeat or first incomplete measure will not have a measure number. It is considered part of the final measure (the last incomplete measure) when counting measures.

So, while it looks like there are 9 measures in this melody, there are only 8 complete measures.

Happy Birthday to You

Hap - py Birth - day   to   You,   Hap - py Birth - day   to   You,   Hap - py

Birth - day   dear   (Name) -   Hap - py Birth - day   to   You!

14. Triplets

Notes normally divide into two or four equal parts.

Triplets can be used to divide a note into three equal parts.

Triplets are indicated as three notes enclosed in square brackets and marked with the number 3.

Quarter note = Two eighth notes = Three eighth-note triplets

Wedding March ▶

Felix Mendelssohn

First and Second Endings

1.

2.

A repeated passage is to be played with a different ending on the second time.

Play from measure 1–6, then play the first ending of measure 7–8. Since there are repeat dots, go back to the beginning and play measures 1–6, and then play the second ending, measures 9–10.

Jingle Bells

Jin - gle bells,   jin - gle bells,   jin - gle all   the

way!   Oh, what fun   it   is   to   ride   in   a

1.

one   horse   o - pen   sleigh!   Hey!

2.

one - horse   o - pen   sleigh!

The Note B♭

Pages 76–78

These exercises are designed to train articulation, combining both tonguing and slurring:

1 ▶ F G A B♭ C B♭ A G   F G A B♭ C B♭ A G   V

Tongued — Slurred — Tongued — Slurred — All Tongued

2 ▶

3 ▶

4 ▶

76

Finlandia

Jean Sibelius

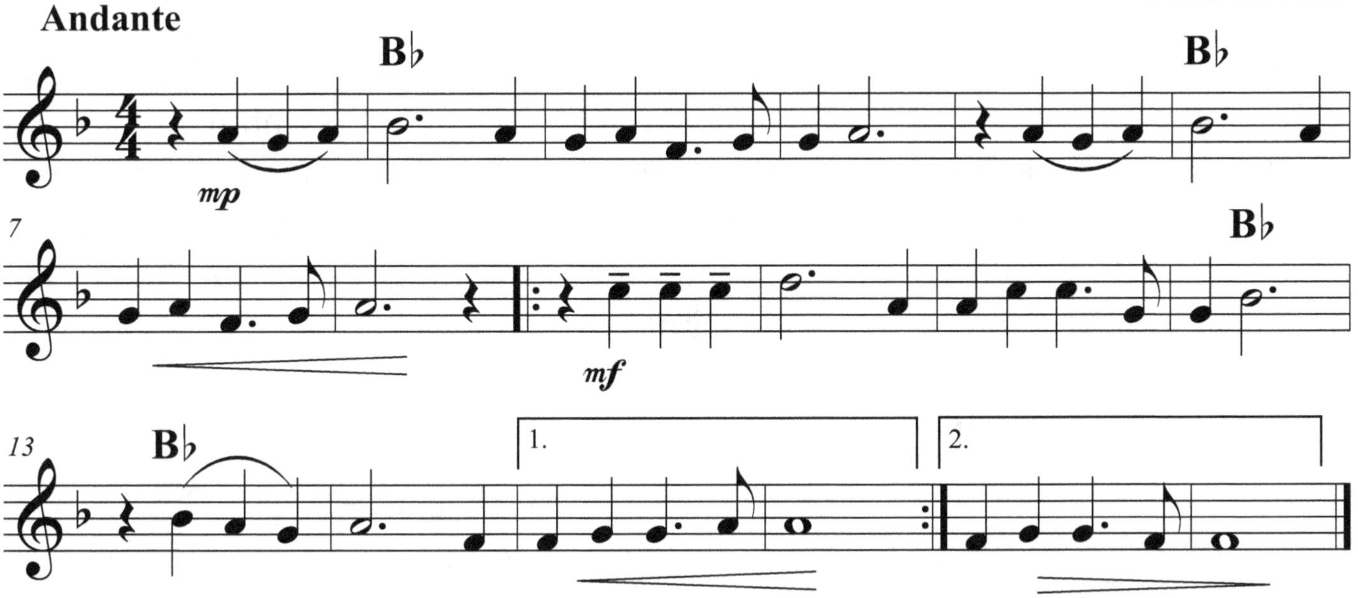

Tiger Rag

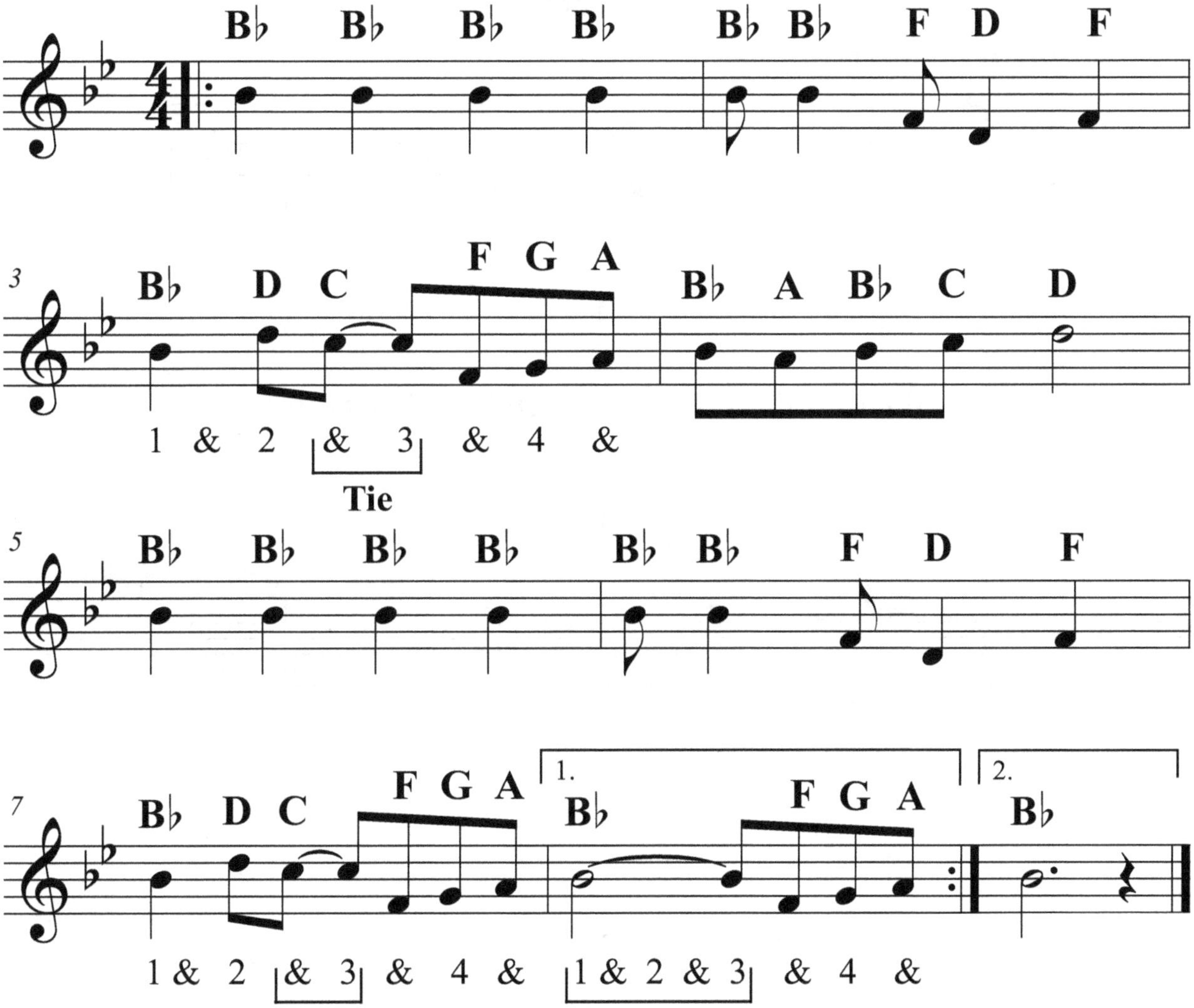

15. 8va in Music

Sign 8va − − − is used for convenience of reading musical notation. This makes playing notes easier and faster. An 8va is a musical symbol used to tell you to play the exact same notes as written, but either an octave (an octave is 8 notes) either higher or lower. The 8va sign simplifies written music for the composer. Instead of having multiple ledger lines extending higher and higher up, the music can be written much more simply with an 8va.

written with 8va written with ledger lines

equals

Play an octave higher

Swanee ▶

Play an octave higher

Written differently, but played the same

16. Tempo

Tempo is a word meaning "tempo of speed", i.e., how fast or slow to play the music.

You must learn to play a piece of music at different tempos. To truly master your instrument, you must be able to play as convincingly at high speed as at low speed, and vice versa. Usually, musicians practice playing at different tempos, and a device such as a metronome helps them do this.

A metronome is a device that produces a click at a regular interval of time. Mechanical metronomes have a pendulum that swings back and forth. You can also use an electronic metronome, or even a metronome app on your phone. If you play an electronic piano, then it should have a function called "Metronome".

For example, one click is equal to one quarter note. Thus, in the 4/4 meter (the most common time signature), each metronome click equals one quarter note, and four clicks equal a full bar.

If you see the designation above the notes that 1 quarter equals 60, then the metronome should make 60 beats per minute, that is, one beat is synchronic with a second. In this case, 1 beat of the metronome is a quarter note.

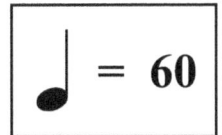

$$\quarternote = 60$$

You can select a different duration for 1 beat of the metronome. Sometimes it is preferred that metronome clicks represent an eighth note, a dotted quarter note, or a half note.

$$\quarternote . = 50$$

1 metronome beat is equal to ♩.
50 beats per minute

$$\halfnote . = 60$$

1 metronome beat is equal to 𝅗𝅥.
60 beats per minute

But usually they indicate a quarter note (1 beat of the metronome). It is more convenient if the tempo is not very fast. It is often set to ♩ = 90, 120, 140 beats per minute, but you can set the tempo that suits you. A metronome can help you keep a consistent tempo so that you won't inadvertently speed up or slow down.

Italian Tempo Markings

Italian	English	Beats per Minute
Presto	Very fast	168–208
Allegro	Fast	120–168
Moderato	Moderate speed	108–120
Andante	Moderate walking speed	76–108
Adagio	Slow (at ease)	66–76
Largo	Slow and solemn	40–66

17. Dynamics

Dynamics in music refer to how loud or soft the music is played.

Since the first musicians who began attempting to write music were Italian, the musical terms they created are still used today. So now when you look at music, you will discover a lot of Italian terms and writing.

List of Dynamics

Symbol	Italian	English
ppp	*pianississimo*	Very, very soft
pp	*pianissimo*	Very soft
p	*piano*	Soft
mp	*mezzo piano*	Moderately soft
mf	*mezzo forte*	Moderately loud
f	*forte*	Loud
ff	*fortissimo*	Very loud
fff	*fortississimo*	Very, very loud
<	*crescendo*	Gradually get louder
>	*diminuendo*	Gradually get softer
♩	*accent*	Play much louder
sfz	*sforzando*	Put extra emphasis on a note

The Character of the Tone

The flute has a very beautiful, mesmerizing tone that can range from soft and velvety to vibrant or even sharp. Depending on the musical genre, the tone of the instrument will also vary. For example, classical music requires a smoother, warmer sound. Modern, pop or jazz music requires a cooler tone with some grit. With the flute, the way air is breathed into the instrument's riser plays an important role in the character of the flute's tone. Naturally, the manner of playing is also very important, including articulation and sound production. There are many ways to play the same note (soft, sharp attack, increasing or decreasing the volume of the sound during one note, soft or short release, added grace notes).

A huge role in shaping the flute's tone is played by the performer's own ideas about how the instrument should sound. To develop this ability, you should listen to famous performers and choose a way of playing that suits your taste, creating your own style, since everyone has a special and unique sound. Constantly look for your own tone — the one that will set you apart from other performers. The saddest thing is when someone plays with a weak, hollow, boring tone. It is very similar to when an artist uses only gray paint from a palette, or a singer sings in a sad, quiet, indifferent voice. The sound of the flute is often compared to coloratura soprano or birdsong because of its intonation characteristics and an expressive vibrato. Intonation in speech and intonation in music are very important expressive means that help the author and player to convey the main idea of the piece to the listener.

Why is it Good to Sing?

Sing your favorite songs whenever possible. Sing using different syllables (tah, too, tee, bee, etc.) to match whatever you play on your flute even if there are no words in the melody. That's why this book has so many songs with words. The melody is singable and you can feel the logical structure and movement of musical idea in the phrases. The more and more freely you sing, the more natural and singable the instrument will sound afterward. The flute is an extension of your voice, with your breath and tongue taking the lead and the riser replacing your vocal cords.

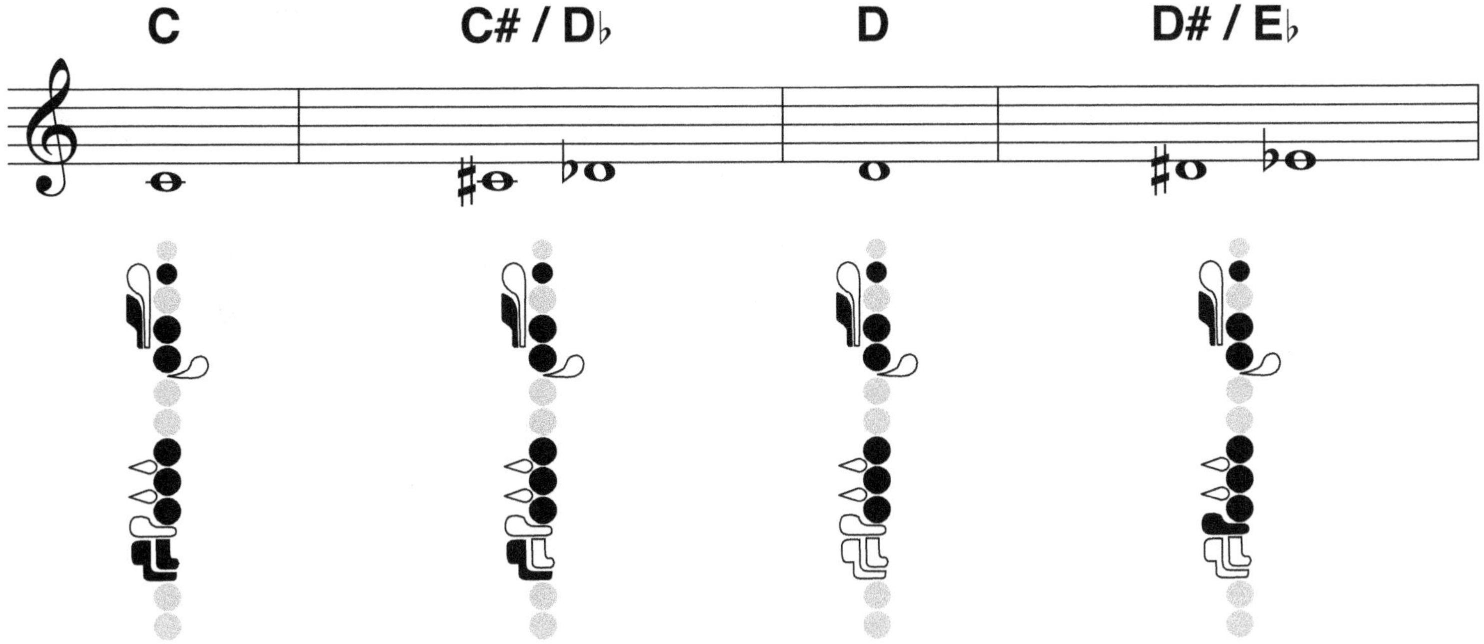
C
C# / D♭
D
D# / E♭

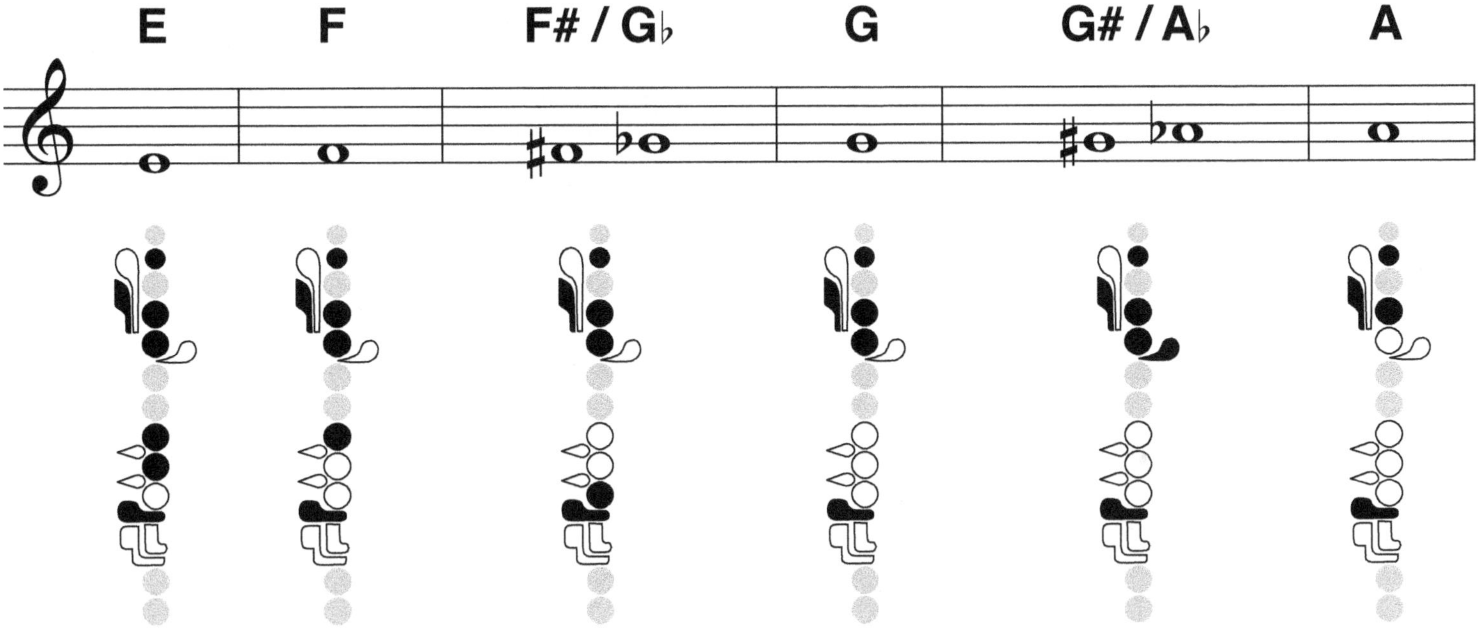
E
F
F# / G♭
G
G# / A♭
A

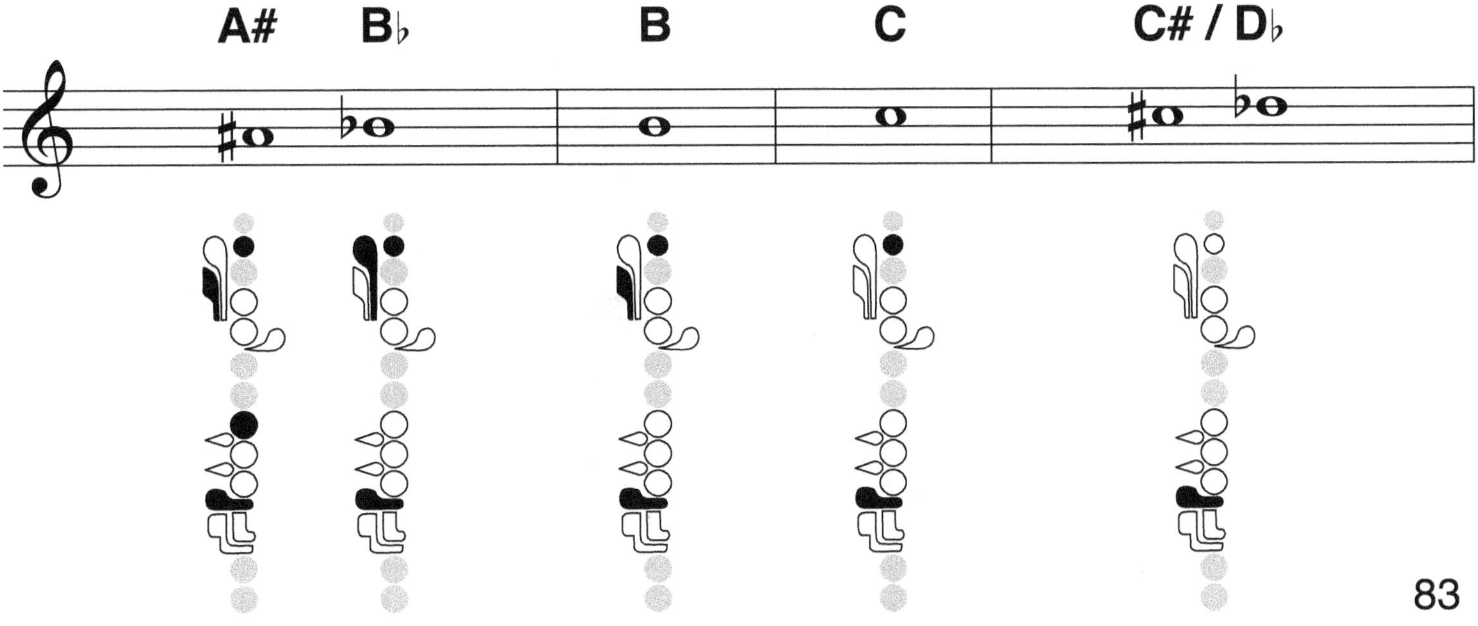
A#
B♭
B
C
C# / D♭

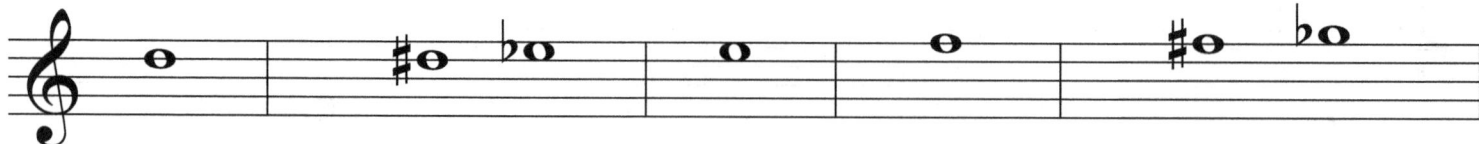

D   **D# / E♭**   **E**   **F**   **F# / G♭**

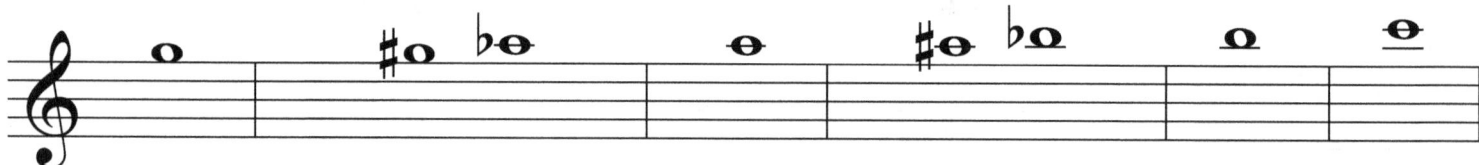

G   **G# / A♭**   **A**   **A#**   **B♭**   **B**   **C**

   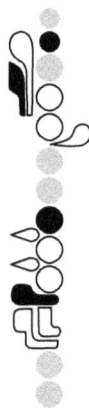   

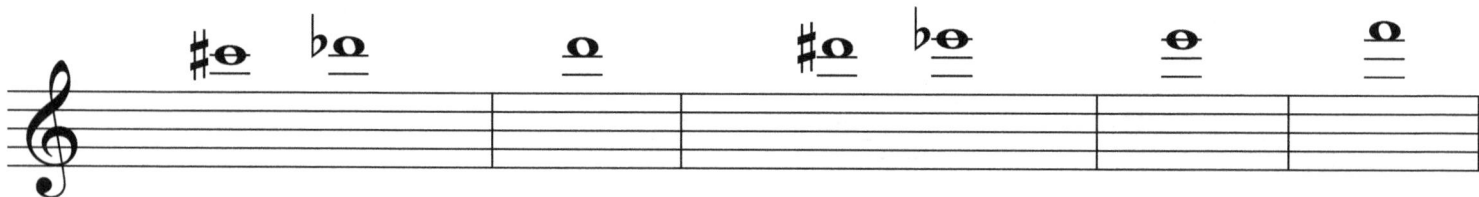

C# / D♭   **D**   **D# / E♭**   **E**   **F**

84

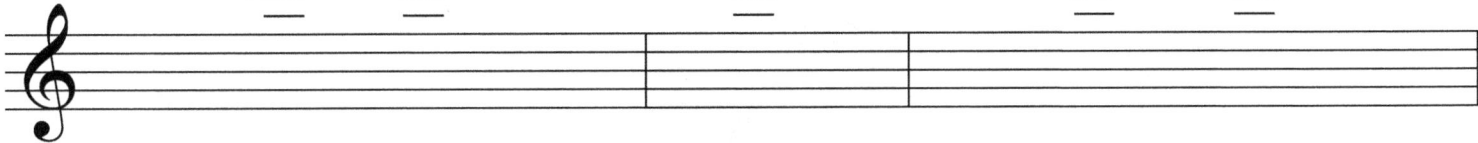

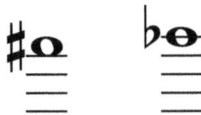

You can download the PDF *(Fingering Chart)* via a direct link:
cutt.ly/ZrmHVgff
or scan the QR code:

PART 3 ▶

Pages 89–110

For any questions, comments or suggestions, email us at:
avgustaudartseva@gmail.com

Scarborough Fair ▶

Traditional

A   A   E   E   B   C   B

Are   you   going   to   Scar - bo-rough

A   E   G   A   G

Fair?   Pars - ley,   sage,   rose -

E   F#   D   E   A   A   A

ma - ry   and   thyme.   Re - mem - ber

G   E   E   D   C   B   G   G

me   to   one   who   lives   there, ___   For

A   E   D   C   B   A   G   A

once   she   was   a   true   love   of   mine.

Red River Valley

Traditional

From this val - ley they say you are go - ing. I will miss your bright eyes and sweet smile For they say you are tak - ing the sun - shine. That has bright - ened our path for a while.

Believe Me, If All Those Endearing Young Charms

Be - lieve me if all those en - dear - ing young charms which I gaze on so fond - ly to - day_____ were to change by to - mor - row and fleet in my arms like__ fair - y gifts fad - ing a - way._____

Beautiful Dreamer ▶

Stephen C. Foster

Moderato

Beau - ti - ful dream - er, wake un - to me,

Star - light and dew-drops are wait - ing for thee;

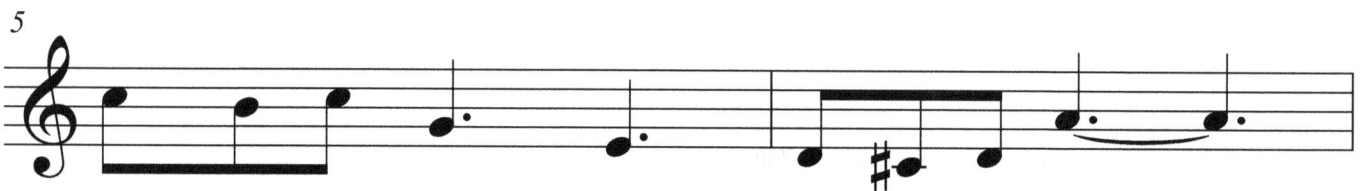

Sounds of the rude world heard in the day,

Lull'd by the moon-light have all pass'd a - way!

Beau - ti - ful dream - er, queen of my song,

List while I woo thee with soft me - lo - dy;

Gone   are   the   cares   of   life's bu - sythrong,

Beau - ti - ful dream - er,   a - wake un - to   me!

Beau - ti - ful dream - er,   a - wake un - to   me!

Page 92

Sweet Betsy from Pike ▶

American Ballad

Moderato

Oh, don't you re - mem-ber Sweet Bet-sy from Pike, who

crossed the big moun-tains with her lov-er Ike? With two yoke of

cat - tle a large yel-low dog, A tall Shang-hai roos-ter, and

one spot-ted hog. Say-ing good-bye, Pike Coun-ty fare-well for a

while. We'll come back a - gain When we've panned out our pile.

Page 94

94

Danny Boy ▶

Traditional Irish
lyrics by Fred E. Weatherly

Moderato

Oh Dan-ny Boy, the pipes, the pipes are call - ing. From glen to

glen, and down the moun-tain side, the sum-mer's gone, and all the ro-ses

fall ing. It's you, it's you must go and I must

bide. But come ye back when sum-mer's in the

mea dow. Or when the val - ley's hushed and white with

snow. 'Tis I'll be here in sun - shine or in

sha - dow.__ Oh Dan-ny Boy, oh Dan-ny Boy I love you so.

Songs with Accompaniment

Page 96

Aloha 'Oe ▶

Lili'uokalani

Ha-a - heo Ka u - a-i-na

pa — li Ke nihi a - e-la i ka-na he — le E ha-

ha — i a - na i - ka li — ko Pu-a a - hi-hi le-hu-a o

u - ka A - lo-ha oe a - lo-ha oe E - ke

o - na-o-na no-ho i - ka li — po A fond em - brace a

ho-i a - e au Un - til we meet a - gain. Ha-a gain.

Down in the Valley ▶

American folk song

Adagio

Down in the Val - ley, Val - ley so

low, _____ Hang your head ov -

er, hear the wind blow. _____

Hear the wind blow, dear, hear the wind

blow, _____ Hang you head ov -

er, hear the wind blow. _____

Page 97

Hello! Ma Baby ▶

Howard and Emerson

Moderato

I've got a lit-tle ba-by, but she's out of sight, I talk to her a-cross the tel-e-phone;___ I've nev-er seen my hon-ey but she's mine all right; So take my tip and leave this gal a-lone.___ Ev-'ry sin-gle morn-ing, you will hear me yell, "Hey Cen-tral! fix me up a-long the line."___ He con-nects me with ma hon-ey, then I rings the bell, And this is what I say to ba-by mine,___ Hel-lo! ma ba-by, Hel-lo! ma hon-ey, Hel-lo! ma rag-time gal,___

28

Send me a kiss by wire,___ Ba-by my heart's on fire!___

32

If you re-fuse me, Hon-ey, you'll lose me, Then you'll be left a-

35

lone; Oh! ba-by, Tel-e-phone and tell me I'm your

38

1. own. Hel-lo! Hel-lo! Hel-lo! there. 2. own.

Page 98

In the Good Old Summer Time ▶

music by George Evans
lyrics by Ren Shields

Allegro

There's a time in each year that we al-ways hold dear,

Good old sum-mer time; With the birds and the tree-ses and

sweet scen - ted bree - zes, Good old sum - mer

time, When your day's work is o - ver then

you are in clo - ver and life is one beau - ti - ful

rhyme, No trou - ble an - noy - ing, each

one is en - joy - ing, The good old sum - mer

time. In the good old sum - mer time, In the

good old sum - mer time, Strol - ling thro' the sha - dy

lanes, With your ba - by mine; You hold her hand and

she holds yours. And that's a ve - ry good sign That

1.

she's your toot - sey woot - sey in The good old sum - mer time.

2.

In the time.

Page 100

101

Let Him Go, Let Him Tarry ▶

Traditional Irish

♩ = 80

7

Now Brid-get was a Col-leen with an

in - de-pen-dent air, And Brid-get had a sweet-heart who was

gay and de-bon - air, He would woo her, court her jilt her near - ly

ev - ry oth - er day, Till fi - nal - ly Miss Brid-get was

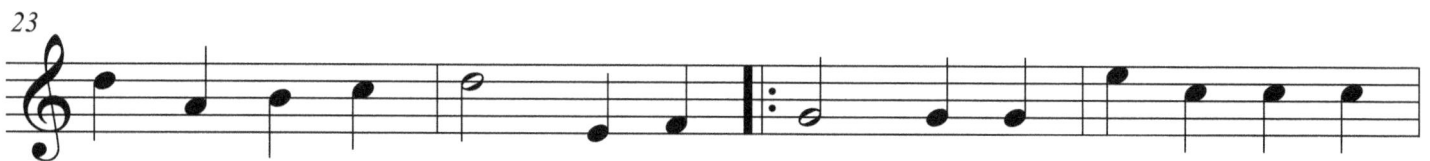

heard, at last to say. Let him go, ler him tar - ry, let him

sink, or let him swim, He does - n't care for me, And

I don't care for him, He can go and get an - oth - er, That I

35 hope he will en - joy. For I'm goin' to - mar - ry A

39 far nic - er boy. Let him go, let him

43 go. Let him go, let him tar - ry, let him

47 stay, He can go, and get an - oth - er That I

51 hope he will en - joy, For I'm going to mar - ry A

55 far nic - er Boy   **1.**   Let him Boy. **2.**

Page 102

Let My People Go ▶

Negro spiritual

Moderato

When Is - rael was in E - gypt land,___ Let my peo-ple go,
need not al - ways weep and mourn,

___ Op - pressed so hard they could not stand,
And wear these slav - 'ry chains for - lorn,

Let my peo - ple go,___ Go down___

Mo - ses___ Way down in E - gypt land,___

Tell old___ Pha - raoh, Let my peo - ple go.___ We

Page 104

The Man I Love ▶

George Gershwin

Tea for Two ▶

Vincent Youmans

Page 106

Wade in the Water ▶

Traditional song

Swing! ♩♩ = ♩♪³

Wade   in the wa - ter,   Wade   in the

wa - ter child - ren. Wade   in the wa - ter

God's gonna trouble the   water.   Who's all those   children all

dressed   in red?   God's   gon - na trou - ble the   wa - ter.

Must be the   one that Moses   led.   God's gonna trouble the   wa -

ter.

108

Wade in the

wa - ter, ___ Wade in the wa - ter child - ren.

Wade in the wa - ter God's gonna trouble the wa - ter.

Page 108

Ja-Da

Bob Carleton

Ja - da ___ Ja - da ___ Ja-da Ja-da Jing, Jing, Jing. ___ Ja - da ___ Ja - da

Ja - da Ja - da Jing, Jing, ___ Jing.

That's a fun - ny lit - tle bit of me - lo - dy,

It's so soo - thing and ap - peal - ling to me, It goes

Ja - da ___ Ja - da ___ Ja-da Ja-da Jing, Jing,

Jing, Oh yeah! Ja-da Ja-da Jing, Jing, Jing!

Scales and Diatonic Modes

In traditional classical music, the 7-note major sequence is called the major scale (the character of the sequence is cheerful). It is built according to the following pattern:

whole step + whole step + half a tone + whole step + whole step + whole step + half a tone: C D E F G A B

C Major

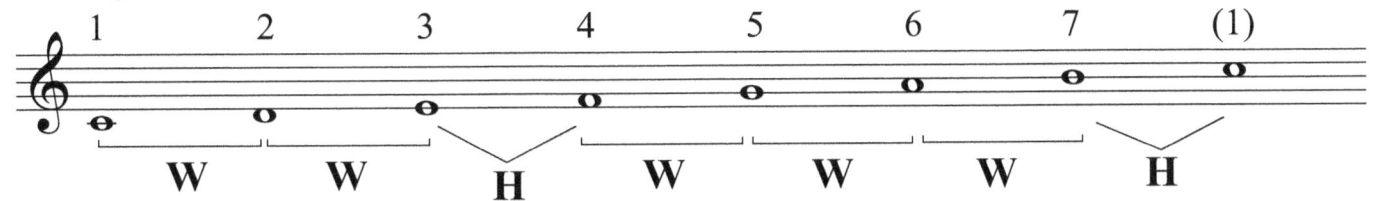

The minor scale (which means that the character of the sound sequence is sad) is built according to the pattern:

whole step + half a tone + whole step + whole step + half a tone + whole step + whole step: A B C D E F G

A minor

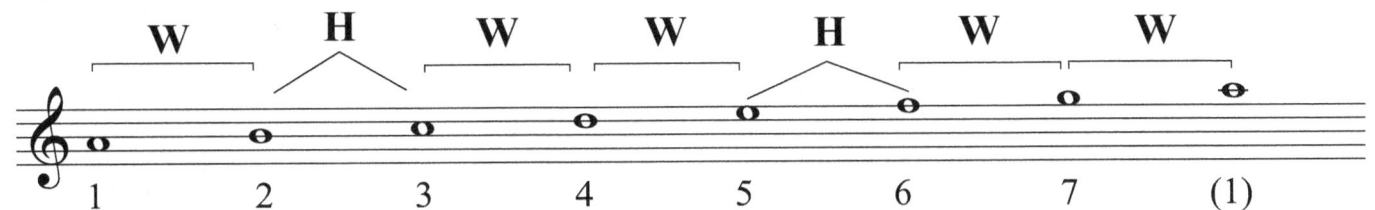

To understand how certain key symbols are used, you need to recognize that the composer first chooses a major or minor key for their piece. Then the sharp and flat symbols logically follow from this initial choice. For example, the major key goes W, W, H, W, W, W, H. The minor key has a different structure: W, H, W, W, H, W, W.

Based on this pattern, you can build a scale from any key. There are no sharps or flats in C major and A minor. This is why these are the easiest keys to play in. However, sometimes the composer uses other keys, which may have anywhere from one to three, or even four sharps or flats in the key signature.

You should learn the order of sharps in key signature notation: F♯, C♯, G♯, D♯, A♯, E♯, B♯.

The order of flats in key signature notation is the opposite of sharps: B♭, E♭, A♭, D♭, G♭, C♭, F♭.

Over time, the players memorize the key signatures of all the keys.

For example, in the D major the main note is D. There are two sharps in the key of D major: F♯ and C♯. You can always figure out the number of sharps or flats in a given key using the above pattern, i.e., building step-by-step (W, H) each note, raising (sharp) or lowering (flat) the pitch if necessary.

Circle of Fifths

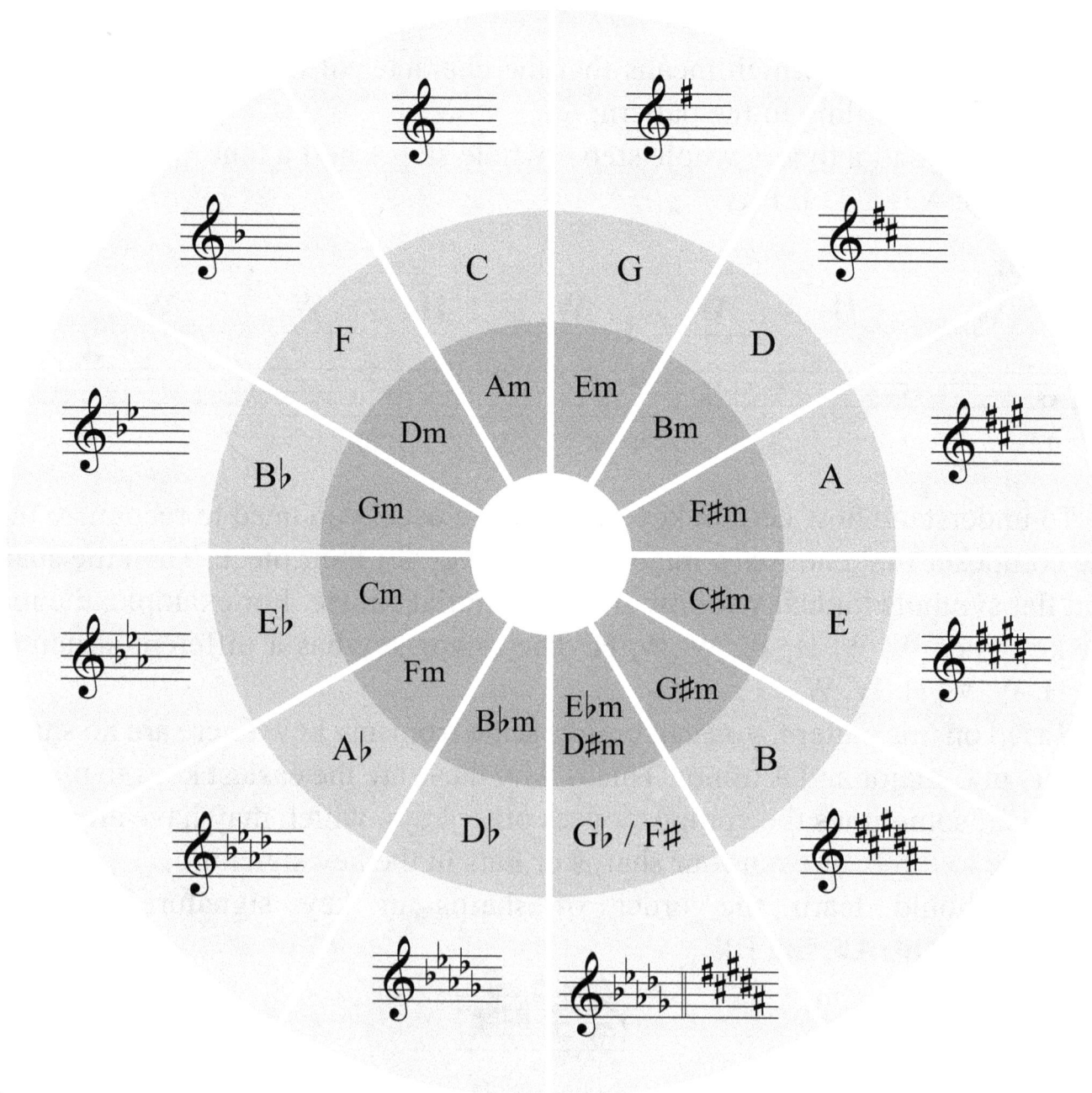

Major and Minor Scales

C Major

C
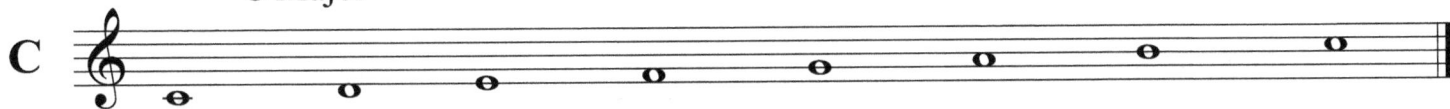

A minor (m)

Am

G Major

G
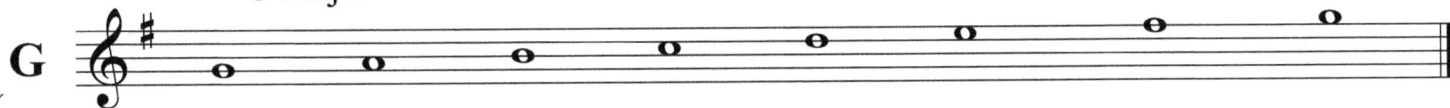

E minor

Em
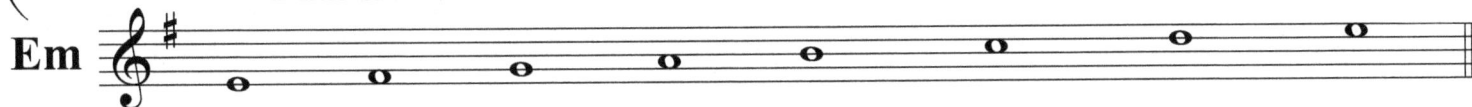

D Major

D
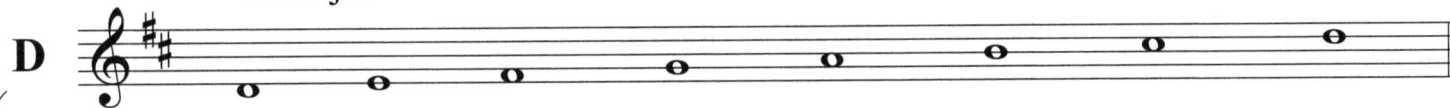

B minor

Bm

A Major

A
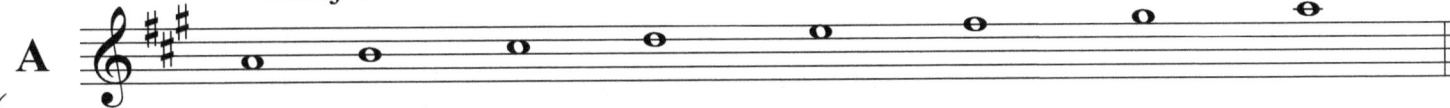

F-sharp minor

F#m
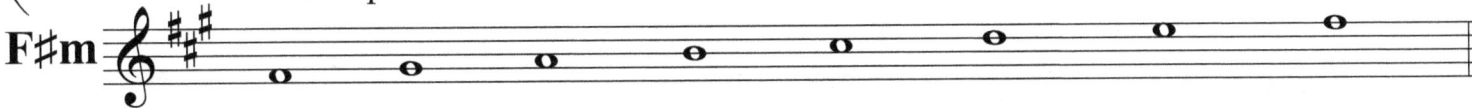

E Major

E

C-sharp minor

C#m
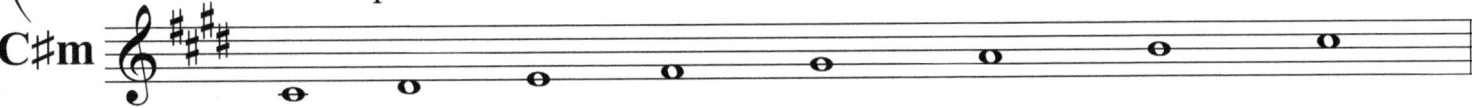

B Major

G-sharp minor

F Major

D minor

B-flat Major

G minor

E-flat Major

C minor

A-flat Major

F minor

D-flat Major

B-flat minor

114

COMPLETE PIANO for Beginners

AVGUSTA UDARTSEVA

COMPLETE PIANO *for Beginners*

Theory and Practice
65 Songs + Video

Learning to play your favorite songs on the piano is easy!

Today the piano is probably the most popular musical instrument in the world. Playing this instrument will give you an unforgettable experience.

The book contains musical theory, practical exercises, and 65 popular songs for adults.

ISBN: 979-8361128570

ASIN: B0BKYHL7PC

United States   **United Kingdom**   **Canada**

EASY RECORDER LESSONS *for Kids*

VIDEO AND AUDIO

60 Songs

First Book Step by Step

- Learning step by step: starting with more simple tunes, then gradually moving to more complex songs;
- Includes music theory, instrument history, practice, recommendations and many entertaining songs;
- Learn the position of the body and hands, how to breathe properly and play easily;
- Letters above each note and simple explanations;
- Convenient large U.S. Letter print size;
- Video accompaniment to all lessons by direct link inside the book;
- 2-in-1 Book: Recorder lessons and video + 60 Songs.

And it's great for adults

ISBN: 979-8386419004

ASIN: B0BXMX7ZVN

United States   **United Kingdom**   **Canada**

www.ingramcontent.com/pod-product-compliance
Lightning Source LLC
Chambersburg PA
CBHW081515040426
42447CB00013B/3232